Dr Berg (Laurence)

Many thanks for your
stalwart support of
my campaign. Please
accept this book as a
small token of my
appreciation. Let's plan
to get together in the
near future.
                All the best,
                    Nik

WAGE
THE
BATTLE

WAGE THE BATTLE

PUTTING AMERICA FIRST IN THE FIGHT TO STOP GLOBALIST
POLITICIANS AND SECURE THE BORDERS

PAUL NEHLEN

 WND Books

WAGE THE BATTLE

Published by WND Books, Washington, D.C. WND Books is a registered trademark of WorldNetDaily.com, Inc. ("WND")

Book designed by Mark Karis

WND Books are available at special discounts for bulk purchases. WND Books also publishes books in electronic formats. For more information call (541) 474-1776, e-mail orders@wndbooks.com or visit www.wndbooks.com.

Hardcover ISBN: 978-1-944229-77-1
eBook ISBN: 978-1-944229-78-8

Library of Congress Cataloging-in-Publication Data available upon request

Printed in the United States of America
17 18 19 20 21 22 LBM 9 8 7 6 5 4 3 2 1

CONTENTS

1

THE WAR ROOM

WE WON BEFORE A SINGLE VOTE WAS COUNTED.

The crowning achievement of my campaign for Congress came a week before Election Day. My communications guy, Noel Fritsch, and I were getting ready to leave our "war room" to head to Madison, Wisconsin, for a live interview with *Fox & Friends*. We were tired, still shaking out the cobwebs from a late-night strategy session. And we were still reeling from our victory the day before.

Paul Ryan had told CNN reporter Manu Raju there were problems with Trans-Pacific Partnership (TPP) and that it would need to be modified before it got a vote. Noel had literally jumped out of his chair when he saw it come up on his news feed, shouting: "Holy sh*t! Holy sh*t. Oh my God, dude. You did it. Ryan caved on TPP!"

It didn't register. I squinted at him, shook my head, and said something to the effect of, "What the hell are you talking about?"

Even now, a day later, I still couldn't fully process it. As Noel filled me in on the details about the upcoming interview, I focused on the task at hand. We had work to do. We had to be somewhere.

We had beaten the TPP, and I couldn't even stop to savor it. As far as I was concerned, the battle wasn't over.

We stepped out of the house into the cool Wisconsin air just before sunrise. The birds were just beginning to sing as I climbed into the black Lincoln that would take us to the interview. But I barely noticed the beautiful morning. My mind was on the intellectual combat to come.

As the car pulled away, Noel and I went into our familiar "interviewer tries to stump the candidate routine," assuming the media would be in attack mode against me. I had done enough interviews to know better than to think *Fox & Friends* would be any different from CNN or MSNBC. They might be friendly, but they would not be friends.

We even discussed the possibility they'd be openly hostile, so I wanted to have a go-to story to put them on their heels. Noel brought up Chris Lace, a Navy sniper who went to Washington to ask Speaker Ryan to work on behalf of veterans. Ryan wanted the opportunity to meet a Navy sniper for the photo op, but

Chris Lace wasn't there to be a prop. He was there to tell Speaker Ryan to put veterans first.

This was perfect because just a few days earlier I had spoken with Al Baldasaro (R-NH), who had a hand in crafting Donald Trump's statement on veterans. Al told me that in the omnibus spending bill Speaker Ryan shepherded through Congress, money had been taken away from veterans.[1]

If the opportunity presented itself in the interview, I'd meld these two stories together to show just what kind of politician Speaker Ryan really is.

Continuing toward Madison, we discussed the TPP trade deal. It may not have been dead yet, but it was severely wounded. Speaker Ryan was also on the defensive on immigration, as outrage built over the ongoing refugee resettlement debacle he had funded. We were seeing mailers from the Ryan campaign claiming he was for securing the border, showing he was sensitive to the charge that he was weak on the issue.

I had to process all this information and mentally distill it into short answers for an interview on live television. Usually, you will get something like five hundred words out of your mouth in the course of an entire interview.

I'm an engineer, a talkative one. I have told the joke a jillion times: "What's the difference between an introverted engineer and an extroverted one? The extroverted one looks at your shoes when he's talking to you."

Fortunately for me, I broke that mold.

We arrived and were sent into the green room in Madison. The room was nothing much, a few Scandinavian leather chairs and a coffee table. But the banal surroundings represented the calm before the battle.

Noel and I went over the issues. I felt good. I had my material. I thought of the volunteers pounding doors all over the district. I was going to be on a national show, which generally translated to a bump in fund-raising.

Let's do this.

I had a ritual. I'd generally listen to one of two songs before going on air:

1. "Moneytalks" by AC/DC.

Ryan represents the girl in the song with the lyrics "Hey little girl. You break the laws. You hustle, you deal, you steal from us all."[2]

2. "One Shot" by Eminem.

When I'm on camera, I'm standing up for all the people who will never have the voice, or a platform, to tell the Paul Ryans of the world what they've done and what they're still doing to America. Over the course of the campaign, I became more and more fired up, and at the same time more professional. Watch my first interview with Neil Cavuto. Then watch this interview with *Fox & Friends*. You'll see the difference.

It's ironic I like this song but at the same time have no respect for Eminem's politics or his view toward law enforcement. Act like a thug, get treated like a thug. The guy has talent, but it's misdirected. I pray he gets his life in order.

In any event, after my preinterview ritual, the door opened to the studio and we headed in. By now, I was familiar with the staff in all the studios in Madison and Milwaukee. Everyone was professional and Wisconsin nice, which is to say really nice, not fake nice.

I hopped in the chair and fixed my tie. The cameraman helped with the earpiece, and soon I was talking to the control room in New York, along with whoever wandered into the room as the lights fired up. They checked my face for any glare, hitting me with some powder to bring the shine down to a respectable level. And as all these little rites and rituals were going on, the tension was rising.

Doing a live TV hit is pure adrenaline. You are looking into a camera ten to fifteen feet away. That camera is your world. You don't dare look anywhere else, lest you look like a whacko bird. There may be a live TV screen with the interviewer, but that is only a distraction. Moving and gesticulating is fine, and it actually beats sitting still (as I found out the hard way with the Cavuto interview very early on). But you don't dare look away from that camera.

The most important thing you learn is that you are talking to the audience, not the interviewer(s). Your message has to be succinct. It is more important than the narrative the interviewer wants to promote. Blocking and bridging to your message is the only way to get it to the viewer.

I'll answer any question asked. That isn't the issue. The issue is you only have five hundred words. If they are all wasted on nonissues, you've failed the interview.

Three minutes before go time. Last sound check. Lighting good. All good. Control rooms want you to be ready and not drinking water or playing around. The last thing they (or you) want is you being filmed with your finger in your ear. You laugh, but imagine that happening in front of three million people.

This was the quiet zone. I took a moment to thank God for the opportunity to make a difference in the world. I asked Him to let the words that would come out of my mouth be His words. The truth.

Last contact with control room was at thirty seconds. I'd been listening to the show in the earpiece for the last ten to fifteen minutes so I'd know who was on and what the subject matter was. You can work that into an answer, essentially building on and reinforcing the topic, or you can rebut it, refuting what the previous guest had to say.

And then, we were on.

We were live, and I could hear Steve Doocy introducing me on the air as Paul Ryan's Republican challenger in Wisconsin's First Congressional District. Steve went on past the intro to say something to the effect that Speaker Ryan had been on the show many times, and I thought to myself, *Is he trying to intimidate me?* Then Steve said that Fox had invited Speaker Ryan to be on with me, and Speaker Ryan had declined the invite.

"So, *who* are you?" he asked in a terribly condescending tone.

Right off the bat, gloves off.

I responded that I'm just a guy, and just like everyone else, I'd be judged by what I do and who I hang out with. "So I'm here to share a quick story about a guy named Chris Lace."

I gave the three interviewers the story about Chris and fused it into how Speaker Ryan's omnibus bill had transferred money away from veterans to illegal aliens.

I couldn't see the three interviewers on the couch, but I had caused a collective meltdown.

"What do you mean he took money away from veterans?" they asked.

"It's a matter of public record," I replied. And I was absolutely right.

I then went on to talk about Ryan's engineering of the Puerto Rico bailout and his close ties to Cesar Conda, Marco Rubio's former chief of staff and an advocate for mass immigration. I pointed out that Speaker Ryan's top aide is Dan Senor, a Never Trumper who compared Trump to Hitler. They asked something about Trump and Ryan's relationship, and I simply stated that I was not surprised that Mr. Trump wasn't "quite there yet," using Paul Ryan's words against Trump back against Ryan.

We had a bit more back-and-forth, and I brought up the "fake news" controversy about the Khan family. And I made sure to mention that I'd written a well-researched article praised by Donald Trump in a tweet, and I had responded to the Republican nominee "No problem."

The interview ended, and I felt I had just landed some good blows against Speaker Ryan and his omnibus bill. I had also tied myself to Trump, the leader of the party. While we didn't talk about TPP, the collapse of border security, the manufactured refugee crisis Speaker Ryan fully funded and supported, or Ryan's threat to sue Donald Trump over admitting Muslims to the United States, I still thought I had hit on some important issues.

Back at the war room, my team's initial reaction was mixed. They weren't aware I'd spoken with Al Baldasaro about the omnibus funds being taken away from veterans.[3] When I told them I had the evidence to back up my claims, I was the hero. The reality was that Al was the hero. If it weren't for him telling me about the situation, I wouldn't have been able to use it against Ryan.

That interview stuck with me on Election Day. We'd set up our Election Day operation in in the Janesville, Wisconsin, hotel Ryan usually reserved. It fit with the area we were focused on in the final push. Surprisingly, Ryan's team hadn't bothered to secure the venue, and we were grateful to have a location with sufficient rooms for out-of-town guests.

I talked with staffers as the returns came in. The mood was high and spirits were good. We had worked so damn hard in the scant four and a half months since I had announced my candidacy. I had made the announcement at the beginning of April, and since then, it had felt like sprinting a marathon.

I'm not sure why I kept coming back to that interview that night. I suppose it was because it had focused on how Speaker Ryan, and by extension our entire national elite, was selling out the very people who most deserve our respect and protection.

I thought of the speech we had prepared. It wasn't a victory speech or a concession. It was a call to action.

Winning the seat would just be icing on the cake. I wasn't supposed to win. In Wisconsin, only one incumbent federal representative has lost a primary race since 1950. That's one race in thirty-three over the past sixty-six years. If that weren't enough, I was running against not just some random congressman, but the sitting Speaker of the U.S. House of Representatives.

My campaign manager entered the room, white as a ghost. I asked if everything was okay. He sat down and said, "It's over. Ryan has you by a huge margin."

I took a huge breath and let it out. Then I smiled.

"We won," I said. "We beat TPP. Let's go out there and give them one hell of a speech."

And that's exactly what we did.

So here and now, I call you to battle again.

As we enter the next phase of this war for America, let's not forget the monumental achievement of this campaign: We stopped the Trans-Pacific Partnership. Let that sink in. We changed the course of American history for the better.

Twelve nations negotiated for over half a decade. The treaty was kept in a locked bunker. TPP was lauded more than forty times by Hillary Clinton as the gold standard for trade deals. President Obama lobbied for this awful globalist nightmare of a treaty.

And we stopped it.

And by "we," I mean everyday, grassroots people. I'm not a politician. I'm a manufacturing guy. I'm an engineer with an MBA. At heart, I'm a small-town Midwestern man who loves his country. I fight for the people who show up for work every day and want to believe that if they work hard, they too can live a peaceful life, free from the tyranny of globalism, because their elected leaders will labor on their behalf.

But I saw that wasn't happening. I saw our way of life at risk. So, I stepped up to the microphone and delivered a righteous message to America.

Every single one of you has that inside you.

If you reject the mainstream media fake news, get red pilled to the truth, roll up your sleeves, and wage the battle, there is nothing you can't accomplish.

Trust me on this. Humbly speaking truth to power works. You could be the next lightning rod of good in your community if you put your mind to it.

America is unique. She is worth fighting for. Wage the battle.

2

BREAKING ONTO THE SCENE

I'M A SON OF THE MIDWEST, the American heartland. But though I was occasionally smeared as an "isolationist" during the congressional campaign, I've traveled all over the world. And what I saw around the globe during my career in manufacturing shaped the nationalist beliefs I have today.

I worked for a series of Fortune-level firms, a job that took me to many nations. I moved my family roughly every two years, sometimes more than that, as I climbed the ladder with SPX Corporation. I completed my MBA in 2005 and worked for the company in North Carolina, Florida, Wisconsin, Texas, Michigan, London, the Middle East, and Africa. I left in 2013 to work for another global manufacturer.

Though business is global, I learned pretty damn quickly how important the nation-state still is. The EU is not the United States of Europe. Every country has a favorite country to hate: the Brits hate the Danes, the Danes hate the Germans and the Brits, and almost everyone hates the French. The Poles for the most part didn't really hate anyone and are some of the hardest-working, smartest, kindest, funniest folks you'd want to meet. I made lifelong friends everywhere I went and was amused when they suggested Americans were racists—and couldn't see the pure ethnocentrism that drove their own actions.

For example, the first time I drove from Germany to Denmark, I was with a Brit and another American. As we crossed into Denmark, I remarked, "Wow. It looks just like a Christmas wonderland."

"Ack! Nonsense," shot back the Brit from the backseat. "There's Danes here."

On another occasion, I was leading a meeting in Germany with two of the general managers there and suggested we contact some of our supply-chain people in Évreux, France. Almost simultaneously the Germans said, "Herr Nehlen, why would you ruin a perfectly good day by speaking to a Frenchman?" Funny stuff. In the end, we pulled together and got the job done.

Breaking into the political scene was different from operating in the business community. I'd already developed a strong business network after nearly thirty years in the trenches. That is not what wins elections. I knew I had to meet some powerful influencers before I challenged the man second in line to the presidency if I wanted to avoid the pitfalls that had destroyed so many others.

It was the hand of God that directed my first e-mail to a gentleman in Green Bay, Wisconsin. That e-mail eventually led to phone calls with a couple of the key people behind Dave Brat's successful bid to unseat Eric Cantor.

One of those calls led to a dinner in New York City in early January with a man from Virginia. That man is one of the greatest patriots alive today: Ron Maxwell. If you've not seen his films or read his writings, I implore you to do so. Ron is a selfless mentor, and I'm deeply grateful for his guidance, which I mostly follow, and his friendship, which I'll always cherish.

At the dinner in New York City, we discussed my policy positions, and I expressed my sincere desire for Donald Trump to be our next president. Two weeks later, Ron arranged a dinner party at a friend's home in DC. I was given an address and told the appointed hour to arrive. I was not told whose home it was or who would attend. How's that for building anticipation?

I was the first to arrive and looked around nervously. I won't share with you whose home it was because many guests wanted to maintain anonymity. Someone from Breitbart was there (no, not Steve Bannon), as well as more than twenty other people, all of whom were involved in national security or politics. And all of them were interested in ousting Paul Ryan from Congress.

To kick off the event, I was told to give a five-minute presentation on my background. I spoke for fifteen minutes (lesson one of politics: learn to stick to the time limits).

When I was done, I got an earful from the guests, who formally introduced themselves and then started giving me some constructive feedback. Some of it related specifically to policy issues that I brought up. "TPP might be difficult to message to the average voter," said one. "Omnibus has to be something you hammer Ryan on day in and day out," urged another. Other feedback was deep in the weeds on refugee resettlement, detailing Paul Ryan's long career as an open borders advocate and the challenge of exposing that for the average voter. One interesting comment came from someone who claimed to have known Ryan from his first days on the Hill. She said Ryan's initial "I'm going to make a difference" earnestness has been transformed into "Hill-speak." It's that style politicians have of speaking in sound bites, an indication that a person has become an empty suit no longer in touch with the listener or even his or her own soul.

"Assuming, of course, he still has one," she said to laughter.

Looking back on this experience, I'm filled with admiration for each one of these figures. They all work hard and have dedicated their lives to fighting for America. And even their criticism was designed to make me a stronger and more effective advocate. After exchanging contact information, I went home, my mind racing. I stayed up well into the night, reading everything they had suggested.

A few weeks after that dinner, I was visiting family in northern Virginia. On my way back to the office, I contacted the Breitbart journalist I had met and said I would love to say hello. That person suggested I meet Steve Bannon.

It's funny how the little details stick with you when you recall important life events. My wife and I were forty minutes out, and since I had been drinking coffee all morning, I needed to get to a rest room when I arrived. We parked a few blocks from Bannon's address and "church-walked" (you know: that double-time walk you do when you're late for church but don't want to be seen sprinting in the parking lot). As we hurriedly ascended the steps, I looked at my wife and said my political career was going to be over before it started because my bladder was going to burst any second. She laughed and told me to be serious. Believe me: I was being serious.

Steve Bannon's office had a huge brass knocker on a massive door. After a few swings, Bannon opened it and greeted me with a firm handshake. This was a man I had revered as the one true voice of the people, countering the lies of the corporate media and the DC political UniParty. And yet, there I was, meeting a genuine hero, and all I wanted was to get to a bathroom!

After answering nature's call, I found that Bannon and my wife had settled at a long, old wooden table. It looked like the formal dining room in the distinguished brownstone blocks from the Supreme Court. I sat between them. Belying these stately surroundings, Bannon bluntly got to the point.

"So you're the guy who's thinking of running against Paul Ryan," he said. "Why would you do that?" I responded that Ryan's support of TPP and his embrace of open borders necessitated a primary challenge.

This was only the beginning of Bannon's machine gun–style interrogation. He drove on relentlessly, asking question after question, with seemingly ten more prepared after I had just finished answering the last one. It was exactly like being grilled on his radio show.

Bannon asked me point-blank who I wanted to be the

next president. Without hesitation, I said, "I'm pulling for Trump." He asked me why. I told him Trump was the only one talking about this terrible Trans-Pacific Partnership and the complete lack of border security. Bannon's one-word response: "Interesting." Bannon then reeled off a few questions related to TPP, I suspect to test my knowledge of the deal, and a few on border security.

He then asked if I knew what the opposition and the media would do to me and my family in terms of digging into my past. He told me they would use half-truths and outright lies to try to destroy me. When I said I understood, he responded bluntly, "No, you don't." Then he turned to my wife and asked what she thought about all this.

I looked at my wife as she earnestly responded that she was concerned people would say horrible things. But while she doesn't follow national politics as Steve and I do, she believed in me and knew I was serious about stopping this trade deal. I was touched by her support and her courage.

Bannon immediately launched into another round of questioning, but I interrupted. I asked if I could take him back to something he said earlier. First I told him that my wife and I had agreed that if I was really going to run against Ryan, she would be in "90 percent support, 10 percent protect" mode. Then I reminded him of his earlier comment, which I somewhat derisively mimicked.

"You know how you said they are going to attack me and my family if I do this?" I asked.

"Yeah." Bannon replied.

I looked him straight in the eye and intoned, "You aren't going to talk me out of doing this."

Bannon paused for a second, glared, and responded challengingly, "I'm not going to talk you out of doing this?"

Now I was fired up. I pointed at Bannon and shot back: "Paul Ryan lied to me. To my face. He hasn't fought Obama on anything of substance. This trade deal gives up U.S. sovereignty. We will be the United States of Asia."

Bannon's whole mood changed; he sat back in his chair, crossed his arms, and said with a grin, "You are going to be Paul Ryan's worst f---ing nightmare."

I laughed. And I knew in my heart that though this would be immeasurably difficult, I would weather the storm.

After a few more minutes of chatting, he showed us to the door. As we stepped outside, Bannon noticed one of his reporters talking on a cell phone, pacing on the sidewalk. "I want to introduce you to Julia Hahn," he said.

"I love your work!" I told her, somewhat gushingly. "My God, you reported from the wall outside of Paul Ryan's house."

She laughed and wished me well.

As my wife and I made our way back to the car, my wife suddenly exploded with anger. She thought Bannon's machine-gun interrogation was rude.

"That's okay," I said. "Besides, I was firing back just as quickly."

When she admitted that she'd been fairly shocked by my rapid-fire responses, I told her I'd felt as if Andrew Breitbart's spirit were in that room, and that he'd been pulling for me.

"I don't know about that," she answered, "but I'm glad *you* felt that way."

I said I was glad too—and especially glad she'd been there to speak to Bannon while I ran to the restroom! We both laughed, and she said, "You are one-of-a-kind Nehlen."

Bannon and I didn't speak again until he interviewed me on his radio show. That was the only time we spoke to each other during the campaign. The day before the election, he interviewed me and said on the air to Ron Maxwell, who happened to be the prior guest, "No matter how this election goes, Nehlen's campaign killed TPP." Bannon asked me how it felt to know I'd changed the course of U.S. history. I said it still hadn't sunk in.

I didn't win the seat. But we won the battle over the trade deal. America is better off for it. But that didn't happen until the final weeks of the campaign. It took months of staying on message. And that message had to be delivered door-to-door in the district as well as broadcast nationally.

All politics is local, as they say. I had some good contacts working behind the scenes to get me audiences with those curious enough to hear me out. And when a group hadn't asked me to come, I simply invited myself in.

For example, the local United Auto Workers in Janesville seemed like a prime opportunity to cross over some of the Democrat voters who had been screwed by NAFTA and just about every other globalist trade deal negotiated in the last thirty years. Because Wisconsin's First Congressional District was an R+3 district (Republican with a +3 lean on the Cook Partisan Voting Index), there was little chance a Democrat would take out Ryan in the general election. For union workers who wanted to stop TPP, I was their only real choice.

And honestly, TPP is a fight bigger than union versus non-union. This battle is bigger than Republican or Democrat. That deal ever passes and you can kiss your union good-bye.

When I met the president of the local union in the front lobby of the hall, he told me a Republican candidate had never before stepped foot inside the building. *Shameful*, I thought. I said as much, too.

He invited me and a few of my team back to his office, where we talked for an hour. Clearly, we were on the same side of the fight when it came to TPP. But he was the captain of a ghost ship there in Janesville. With the exit of General Motors, union workers didn't have much left.

I pushed for an endorsement and left there with the assurance that he would speak to the rest of his team. Unfortunately, he could not come through with a concrete endorsement. What occurred was purely partisan; one member of his leadership team said there was no way he would agree to endorse a Republican. So he caved and got more Paul Ryan. Brilliant move.

I wish I could speak to that union president again. "Tell me," I'd ask, "since August 9, how many times has Paul Ryan fought for your ability to make a living there in Janesville? . . . Hmm. How about in Kenosha? . . . Hmm. Racine? . . . Shocking."

My message to union members is simple. Paul Ryan hasn't really done anything to improve your lot in life, even as Speaker of the House. Yet you refused to endorse the only candidate with a real chance to beat him—and demonstrated skill at creating jobs and opportunities to boot—because you preferred to stay inside the Democrat box. What an incredible missed opportunity.

It's painful to see that closed Janesville GM plant, but I drive by it whenever I am in town to keep my blood to a steady simmer.

I also thought I had a shot with the trade unions. When I met with them, I left with the feeling *These guys get it*. TPP goes through and they will be replaced by cheap labor, who will destroy their ability to put food on the table and a roof over their families' heads.

This is serious business, and I took it straight to them. Honestly, I couldn't care less if a shop or site was union or non-union. Of course, they cared though. Since I'd managed both, I told them I'd preferred a nonunion shop because I listen to my employees and because another layer between me and the workforce didn't seem necessary with my hands-on approach—but ultimately the choice was theirs.

"Get with my program," I said, "and I will work like hell to put an immigration policy in place that works for American workers first. We will not sign any multilateral trade deal, but only a bilateral trade deal that protects American workers."

Once again, we got no official endorsement. But we did build a strong network with hardworking union leaders. We'd have to go with that.

Meeting with the unions was only part of my America First platform. Unions had taken a beating in Wisconsin, but I was also meeting with business leaders, who loathe the unions. What would I tell them if they asked where I stood on unions? I didn't wait for them to ask. I told them that Paul Ryan didn't care if he was eviscerating a union shop or a nonunion shop. In fact, Ryan was going to wipe out both with his embrace of bad trade deals and open borders.

What I was offering was the ability to get out from under the weight of government interference in their business. Ryan has for years talked about cutting regulations. Great. I agree that needs to be done yesterday.

But what have we seen Ryan do? He's outsourced writing

regulations of Congress's laws to the executive branch. Oversight? Ryan couldn't be less concerned with the crushing weight of regulations. I say this because he hasn't mounted a single fight that would demonstrate that he does.

As Speaker of the House, he passed the largest omnibus spending bill in the history of the nation, with no riders to prevent spending on anything that he claims violates his principles. Why? Because Paul Ryan doesn't have principles. He has donors.

I laid out the case before the local business leaders. But you could see the fear and trepidation in their faces when it came time to ask them to get involved. This was a big ask. Wisconsin politics is a tightly bound operation. You go against the powers that be and you can expect all hell to break loose. I suspect it is the same in most parts of the nation. What I had counted on was the willingness of at least some people to put their necks on the line when the time came. The grassroots supporters were there. But the larger business leaders couldn't bring themselves to step out of line.

Still, there was an energized group of people in the district, which steadily grew as the campaign progressed. We had regular meetings around the district, and I took any question asked. There was no equivocation. My positions were firm and direct. Interactions with voters at their homes were equally positive.

But we still had to face the brutal reality. We had essentially four months to get our message out against a career politician holding the highest elected office of any Republican in the nation. And he had one hell of a campaign war chest at his disposal.

Think about what $10.6 *million* will do for you versus a contender that can only raise $1.5 million (which was a huge number in four months) in terms of positive media coverage.

Think of it in terms of two customers going to the local car sales lot. One customer buys two new cars every year. The other customer buys a new car every five years. Who is the sales team going to jump to? What local news team will bite the hand that feeds it more than ten times what the other hand does? Of course, none of them will. That goes for TV, radio, and print. We literally had to set up news conferences outside of the local Wisconsin papers just to force them to cover us.

But though I didn't win the seat from Paul Ryan, we as a nation won by defeating the Trans-Pacific Partnership and by electing Mr. Trump to the presidency. And I know, deep in my heart, Paul Ryan hates the fact that we sank his globalist donors' dream of TPP. I'm equally convinced he is just as upset about President Trump's victory.

This election was never about me, the same way the presidential election was never about Mr. Trump. Neither he nor I created the wave of discontent in the nation. That was the work of career politicians, Paul Ryan chief among them. The campaign against Paul Ryan was a battle of ideas: nationalism versus globalism, securing the borders, an immigration policy that works for America first, good trade deals, and a rejection of the DC UniParty.

Why run? I'll tell you why. Paul Ryan represents everything that is wrong with politics in America. He comes to the district and tells us what we want to hear. He would get on TV and rail against President Obama, only to surrender the power of the purse when Obama requested it. Ryan funded every dangerous refugee resettlement program. He gave taxpayer dollars to Planned Parenthood. He made sure money went to programs that further indoctrinate our children in public schools to hate our history, heritage, founding principles, and Constitution. And though Paul Ryan will never use the word *amnesty*, he is all for rewriting America's immigration laws to grant citizenship to illegal aliens that broke the law to come here.

Above all, I ran against Speaker Paul Ryan to stop TPP. That job-destroying, sovereignty-abolishing, train wreck of a trade deal that would have leveled my entire district was negotiated in secret and sold to the American public as a "free trade deal." It was anything but free trade.

I ran to give a voice to the people in the First Congressional District of Wisconsin, a voice they'd never had before. We ran a righteous campaign that spoke truth to power. Speaker Ryan never did debate me, though I publicly challenged him in online videos, on the radio, in ads, and in letters to his campaign.

One radio host that I'll not name told me that he would be interviewing Ryan at the Rock County 4-H Fair and that he'd ask him about debating me. He had previously brought the matter up to Ryan after I challenged Ryan live on his show and invited him to moderate. When I checked back with him the following day, he said that Ryan's people had told him not to ask about a debate, and so he didn't. What does that tell you about the power of the Speakership, and millions of dollars in a campaign war chest?

The people of the United States have a charlatan as their Speaker of the House.

I met Paul Ryan at a Republican fund-raiser in 2014. I was a "diamond sponsor" of the event and had an opportunity to shake his hand and talk to him about Obamacare and what he said were his priorities. Before we parted, my wife and I had our picture taken with Speaker Ryan. I was filled with optimism that we had someone who would fight for the American worker, for American safety.

But what I learned later was that Paul Ryan was working behind the scenes to whip votes for fast-track approval of trade promotion authority for the Trans-Pacific Partnership. That was sometime in April 2015. I couldn't believe it. I immediately jumped on the computer and fired off an e-mail to Ryan, copied to Wisconsin governor Scott Walker, making the case that TPP would be a job killer for America and usurp her sovereignty.

What happened next was that Ryan was filmed high-fiving and chest bumping when fast track passed Congress.

No. Not on my watch.

I waged the battle for America. I waged the battle for the victims of illegal alien violence. I waged the battle for every deputy, sheriff, border patrol officer, and emergency response worker that would have to deal with dangerous narco-terrorists crossing our southern border and every American that would be a potential target for radical Islamic terrorists that Speaker Ryan was bringing to our shores. I waged the battle for the moms and dads who, under the umbrella of the Remembrance Project, worked on behalf of families who had lost a loved one to illegal alien violence.

Waging the battle meant giving up my life as a manufacturing executive. It meant losing the opportunity to bring jobs to America. It meant shelving my inventions that had earned me several U.S. and foreign patents. It also meant stepping into the public spotlight and subjecting myself to criticism for every private decision I'd ever made and every action I'd ever taken, though I never lived my life as though I was going to run for elected office.

Was it all worth it? You're damn right it was. Especially because of the moms and dads who had lost loved ones to illegal aliens. It was heart-wrenching to hear their stories and know they had no advocate in Washington to channel their loss into action. Ryan certainly wouldn't do it. I felt I had no choice but to try to do it myself.

My wife said to me in the waning days of 2015, "I guess we are going to give up our quiet little life." I replied that we do have a wonderful life, and that God has been so good to us. There have been young men in foxholes who have died for us and never had a nice home. There are so many who never got the chance to be married and to raise children. We owe it to them to make sure the America we grew up in is there for generations to come.

Her response reminded me why I loved her so much. She closed her eyes, hugged me, and said that if that's what I felt I had to do, she was 100 percent with me.

3

BORDER WARS

WHEN YOU SPEND THE VAST MAJORITY of your time at work, you develop a bond with those around you that goes beyond simple politeness. For example, when a coworker loses a family member, it is important that as a leader you are there for support. I always respected Rudy Giuliani's take on it: weddings are optional, but funerals are mandatory."[1]

Well, a member of Congress works for the people of his or her district. You may not know them all personally, but you should do your best to come as close to that ideal as possible. And you had better be there at times of grief and loss, especially when the deaths of family members is caused by dereliction of duty within our own government.

It's easy to lose sight of the ordinary people who suffer the consequences of our disastrous policies. When I was running against Speaker Ryan, I buried myself in policy details. I studied immigration policy, trade policy, national security, and so many other things. I talked about an America First agenda. I understood, in an intellectual, abstract sense, how there was a real disconnect between the nationalist policies our citizens needed and the America Last policies our government imposed.

But I didn't really understand the personal consequences until I got a phone call from the woman running the preeminent advocacy organization for victims of illegal alien crime. My time with Maria Espinoza, cofounder and national director of the Remembrance Project, totally changed my perspective. It was a painful reminder that we are fighting for people, not just policies and protocols.

The Remembrance Project advocates for families whose loved ones were killed by illegal aliens. Their flagship initiative is called the Stolen Lives Quilt. Since 2009, Maria has worked to unite the "stolen lives" families, educating the public on the epidemic of killings across the country and raising awareness about the effects of illegal immigration. It is *not* a victimless crime. Maria believes that current laws should be enforced, that our borders should be protected, and that Americans must be the priority in our own country.

Maria lives in Houston with her husband, Tim. She is the child of an immigrant father and a fifth-generation Texan.

Maria attended Abilene Christian University on a track and field scholarship, where she became an all-American. And she is all-American in every sense of that term. She is a shining example of what an American should be.

Maria reached out to my campaign in April 2016. Campaigning was new for me at the time and I hadn't mentally prepared myself for how groups would constantly be contacting me, sometimes just to get attention. It seemed like an onslaught at first because I was laser focused on trade and national security.

When I first spoke to Maria, I maintained my distance. I honestly hadn't met anyone who had suffered like the families on behalf of which her organization advocates. What I needed was a kick in the pants, a shock to the system so I could truly understand the issue. And that's exactly what I got.

THE BORDER

Being an industry man, I've always been of the mind-set that if you want something done right, you do it yourself. And if you want to understand something completely, you need to investigate for yourself.

Early in my career as a business leader, I was assigned the mission of turning around a failing factory. I didn't know it at the time, but the factory was slated for closure. When I got there, I knew it was a mess.

The best way to understand the details of what's wrong in any given situation is to get out in the "field," in this case, the factory floor. I set up a card table and folding chair in the middle of the factory and taped a cardboard sign to the table that simply read Help Desk. Best move ever. We took that business, which was losing money when I got there in 2005, and turned it around in eighteen months. It is still profitable today. I was the catalyst, but those hard workers were the solution.

The same principles should be applied to border security. I already knew that enforcing existing immigration laws and halting un-vetted refugees from entering the United States are two elements of a successful national security strategy. Of course, these commonsense policies are anathema to Paul Ryan and the Washington elite. Many Wisconsin voters, and voters nationwide, don't realize what an open-borders zealot Paul Ryan is. As far as I was concerned, it was his job as Speaker to make certain the House of Representatives was debating and voting on those bills that would make America safe again. His refusal to allow the Republican majority to secure our border isn't just dereliction of duty; it borders on treason.

Yet it is not just Paul Ryan. Ryan is simply part of an entire governing class that seems to regard national sovereignty as passé and immigration laws as immoral. It was John Adams who defined a republic as "a government of laws, and not of men."[2] The idea that the rule of law must always hold true and that no government official can arbitrarily ignore the law is central to our national identity. President Gerald Ford, just after Watergate, repeated, "Our great republic is a government of laws and not of men."[3]

Yet the same people who will ruin your life if you make a mistake on your tax forms are perfectly content with letting tens of millions of illegal immigrants ignore our laws. For example, Barack Obama unilaterally changed immigration laws to give amnesty to millions of illegal immigrants, or as he put it, "took an action to change the law."[4] And though he was Speaker of the House, Paul Ryan did nothing to reverse this unilateral and illegal action. The fact is that there is a class of people in our government who believe the law simply doesn't matter when it comes to immigration issues. And this class consists of members of both parties.

What after all, is the difference between the immigration policies of Hillary Clinton and Jeb Bush? Or for that matter, between George W. Bush and Barack Obama? Sure, the motivations for Democrats and Republicans to support open borders may be different. Republicans want cheap labor; Democrats want a class of permanent dependents they can count on to pull the lever for their party. But both are committed to putting America last and replacing the current American people. On this most critical of issues, there is no real difference between Nancy Pelosi and Paul Ryan.

But though I knew this intellectually, I needed to see it firsthand. I wanted to know what the issues were on the ground, on the factory floor, if you will.

Brandon Darby at Breitbart had been reporting on the border issue in Texas. To facilitate the first of what would become several trips, I reached out to him. We met in San Antonio and made the drive south to Laredo. On the way there, with the windows down in the Texas heat, we cranked out the Stevie Ray Vaughan, T-Bone Walker, and Lynyrd Skynyrd, among others. Meanwhile, I had the incredible opportunity to discuss with this deeply knowledgeable reporter the history of the immigration issue. So many candidates, especially Republicans, had put border security at the center of their campaign, only to let American citizens down when they got to Washington. When it comes to meeting this most basic responsibility of government, our public officials were not earning their pay.

Upon arriving in Laredo, we met two reporters from other news outlets. They were working undercover to investigate kidnappings at the border. After arriving at the hotel, Brandon suggested I spend some time watching videos that demonstrated the brutality of the Los Zetas, Gulf, and Knights Templar cartels.

You can find these films yourself if you go to Breitbart.com/cartel-chronicles. Even while writing this, I just searched the site and was greeted with Mexican street amputations, shoot-outs with rival cartels and military, abductions, kidnappings of doctors, cops turned robbers, cops turned murderers, and so many other crimes and tragedies. I wouldn't recommend it unless you have a strong stomach. You'll see some of the most despicable acts imaginable. But it is important to see these acts and understand that they are coming to our country unless we secure our border and get control of our immigration policy. It's another reason I'm so grateful Breitbart News is living up to the standards the late Andrew Breitbart established.

But the most vicious videos I saw in Laredo are not on Breitbart. They are too graphic. They were films of cartel members slitting the throats of victims and then finishing the decapitation with a long-handled ax. You would have thought this was an ISIS video if you didn't see the faces of the Mexican cartel members and their victims. The murderers then put the heads of their victims in the middle of their backs for the camera to show their last expression. What a depraved soul in each of these barbarians.

Why watch these gruesome films? Because this is what is actually happening. Brandon and his comrades wanted me to understand what is really facing border communities before we went there. They were right to do so. When we finally headed out at dusk, we were wearing body armor and were well armed.

I began my tour near the Rio Grande, in Laredo. Illegals use inner tubes to cross the border, as the water can be deep enough to submerge a person who is carrying anything or doesn't know how to swim. On the American side of the border, there were slit inner tubes, discarded water bottles, and clothing in the trees.

We stayed out until almost 4 a.m. that first night, patrolling the area amid a lightning storm. The storm reflected the rage I felt beginning to build within me. We also stopped and talked to Border Patrol agents in their vehicles stationed some distance from the border. At least one was a single mom on patrol by herself. I'm not a fan of single patrols of any age or gender. We let them know who we were and said we were on the lookout for illegal crossings. We verified the call numbers for reporting anything and departed. In each case, we were told to be careful.

We had called the contact number for the border patrol station on several occasions to see if we would get a live person. Not one time did we speak to someone on the other end of the line. Don't misunderstand me here—I'm not casting any aspersions on Border Patrol agents. Those agents are already overwhelmed and doing the best they can to accomplish their mission without support from Washington. The Obama administration simply did not provide the resources needed for the Border Patrol to have a live person on the other end of the line.

The next day, we found more evidence of crossings, including vast numbers of items and trash dumped by illegals. We called into the Breitbart Saturday radio show and spoke to Steve Bannon and Alex Marlow. They both quizzed me on what I'd seen firsthand. And I had to admit; the experience changed how I thought about the national security issue we face at the border.

I cannot fathom the bureaucrats in Washington stating the border is secure. I refuse to believe they are arguing in good faith. President Barack Obama and the federal government deliberately and purposefully refused to guard our borders and endangered the lives of all our citizens. As the cartels begin to operate within the United States, our elected officials have blood on their hands.

And that includes Speaker Paul Ryan. Ryan and his sycophants on Wisconsin radio and in the Wisconsin newspapers vilified me for supposedly blaming him for the problem. But where else should Republicans put the blame? He is the Speaker of the House, for crying out loud! Who decides what bills get debated on the floor? Who decides, ultimately, where money is spent? Paul Ryan has the majority, and now he has a president who ran on the central issue of immigration. He could ensure the immigration problem was fixed tomorrow if he willed it. But he doesn't want to solve this problem.

After calling in to the radio show, I drove eight hours from the Laredo sector to the El Paso sector to meet with Sheriff Arvin West and Sheriff Oscar Carrillo of the Hudspeth and Culberson counties of Texas.

About halfway into the drive, I got a text message from an unknown number. The person identified himself as Dan Golvach. He said he had heard of me through Maria Espinoza from the Remembrance Project. He wanted to talk because he blamed Paul Ryan for the death of his son Spencer at the hands of an illegal alien. He wanted Ryan out of the House.

I was in a bad area for having a cell phone conversation. I figured I'd wait until I got to the next gas station to call. Just then another text came in from Dan.

It was a picture . . . of Spencer's grave.

Dan texted me that he wanted Paul Ryan to spend all his Father's Days with him at Spencer's grave.

What do you even say to that?

I pulled over and called Dan. We spoke for an hour. Spencer was a twenty-five-year-old musician who had started his own guitar store. He had been sitting at a red light, waiting for the light to change. That's when illegal alien Victor Reyes pulled alongside Spencer and shot him in the head, murdering him in the very neighborhood Dan had grown up in.

Victor Reyes had been previously convicted on multiple offenses, including burglary and assault, and spent time in American prisons. He had been deported four times. But because of our government's contemptuous indifference toward its own citizens, Reyes had been able to illegally reenter our country each time. He went to the "sanctuary city" of Houston, where the city fathers refuse to enforce American immigration laws, and murdered Spencer.

Just imagine the criminal neglect, bordering on treason, that had to take place to enable this senseless crime. This animal Reyes should not have even been in the country. But to Barack Obama, Nancy Pelosi, and, yes, Paul Ryan, Reyes's "right" to flaunt our laws was more important than Spencer's right to be safe in his own neighborhood.

That was the shock to the system I needed.

Dan told me he would work to get me elected because of my stance on illegal aliens and securing the border. Over my campaign, I would meet other parents who had similarly painful stories of loss. All spoke of their inability to get Washington to even care about enforcing our laws. And the name I heard over and over again as one of the most indifferent to their grief and their pain was Speaker Paul Ryan. Just despicable.

After the call with Dan, I pressed on toward Sierra Blanca, Texas, to meet with the sheriffs and their deputies. Also meeting me was a team of filmmakers chronicling the consequences of an open border through the eyes of law enforcement officers who risk their lives daily.

The next morning, we hopped in pickup trucks and headed to the border. I rode with Sheriff West and took notes as we drove. He told me he was taking me to Jurassic Park—and knowing Texan humor—I said that would be great. I eventually came to understand his joke. Around the next turn was a monstrosity of a border wall that looked as if someone had planted iron spikes in a three-foot concrete foundation.

The absurdity of this "barrier" is that it is only seven miles long. The southern border in that particular Texas county is approximately one hundred miles long. Abutting the Jurassic Park wall was the barbed-wire fencing typical of any ranching operation. Turns out, that's exactly who installed the barbed wire fence. Ranchers did! I guess you could say they were doing the job the American government won't do.

As we were driving to "Jurassic Park," Sheriff West said, "When they say the border is more secure than ever before, maybe they mean the management offices of this BPS [Border Patrol Sector], not the physical security of the border." I can't disagree with that.

Unlike near Laredo, this section of the Rio Grande can barely be called a river. It was inches deep. We shot footage near the water and near the fencing. Another location we hit was a footbridge directly into Mexico. No barrier there! You literally don't even get your boots wet walking across from Mexico, and needless to say, there are no lines for customs!

My eyes were opened WIDE. The misinformation we are fed by bureaucrats about the border is criminal.

For example, we are always told a "wall will not work." But consider: since the fall of the Berlin Wall, more than forty countries around the world have built fences against more than sixty of their neighbors—more than thirty of those decisions were made following 9/11, fifteen of them in 2015.

For instance, Hungary built a wall along her border with Serbia and Croatia. In the fall of 2015 the number of border crossings had exceeded 7,000 illegal aliens per day. When the fence went up October 17, 2015, the influx went down to 870 from 6,353 *only a day earlier*. Illegal border crossing were steadily below forty per day throughout the rest of the month.[5]

ILLEGAL BORDER CROSSINGS IN HUNGARY – OCTOBER 2015

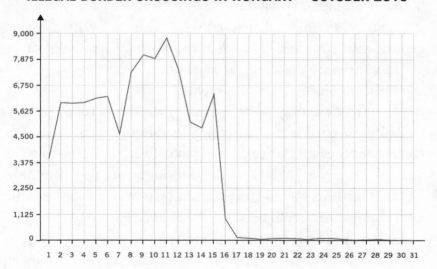

(Hungarian Police/The Daily Caller News Foundation)

Speaking of criminals, the officers in Hudspeth County showed me dash-cam footage of a firefight with drug smugglers. There were drugs in three SUVs being driven by cartel members on American soil. After giving chase, Border Patrol officers apprehended one SUV, another made it across the river into Mexico, and a third got stuck on the riverbank. A shootout ensued. One of our Border Patrol officers was shot and someone radioed for backup.

Did management send backup? No! They said pull back.

Well, one agent said he was not going to leave the other agent there by herself, shot as she was in the leg. More local Hudspeth officers showed up on our side, and Mexican military showed up on their side—driving a military Humvee—given to them by our government! I watched in horror as one officer in the video was forced to engage *with his sidearm.* Meanwhile, on the other side, we had the Mexican army shooting across the border with high-powered rifles.

Luckily, the officer survived. I asked him, "Why did you get out with your handgun when you were up against rifles?"

His answer? "We don't all have rifles."

I just shook my head in disbelief.

Later that evening, while discussing the day's events, we concluded we needed to do something so these guys could get the equipment they needed to do their job. The Texas Department of Public Safety gets $800 million for border security. But only $42,000 made its way to Hudspeth and Culberson counties, and even that had to be split between them. Even Culberson County, which is shaped like an inclined plane with one point touching the border, contains more than thirty-eight hundred square miles of Texas adjacent to the border, containing a prime smuggling route.

My wife and I decided to donate over $45,000 of equipment to those two departments: twenty-five AR rifles, twenty-five sets of body armor, ammo, two drones, and several thermal imaging night vision units. We wish we could have done more.

I made more trips to the border, continued my investigation of border security, and expanded my network of contacts. Sheriff Oscar Carrillo took me to a ranch on the border where the owner told me stories about finding groups of as many as ten children making their way north through the border. He told me much of the violence is caused by cartels telling their drug mules that if they do not resist arrest by whatever means possible, the cartel will chop off their grandmother's fingers back home in Mexico.[6] The days are long gone when smugglers would surrender without a fight.

The "push factor" of the cartels causes the smugglers to run from law enforcement. Not surprisingly, pursuits are up and smugglers are now carrying weapons, both of which endanger law enforcement officers. And if that weren't enough, the Mexican Border Patrol is brutal to the people coming through, shaking down migrants and enforcing the code of the cartels.

Migration is also driving the opiate crisis in this country. Some of it is of course driven by overprescription. But I believe illegal heroin brought across the border is the primary driver. And the attempt by public officials like President Obama and Speaker Ryan to pin all the blame on "overprescription" is just an attempt to avoid this reality.

A senior agent within the National Association of Retired Border Patrol Officers who spent over twenty-six years in the service, red pilled me on what may be really behind America's heroin problem. He believes Mexico's shift from marijuana to heroin production and the push to legalize marijuana supports very powerful DC interests. It's simply a reality that the drug cartels now operate in three thousand American cities.[7]

Obviously, I can't confirm that report. But I can see the curious way Congress is handling the problem. Congress acted quickly to expedite "opiate abuse legislation," which simply treated a smaller cause (abuse of prescription drugs) of the larger drug problem. But it has shown no willingness to cut off the record supply of cheap Mexican heroin. Indeed, as chronicled in the shocking documentary *Death by Fentanyl*, the Mexican cartels paid Chinese chemists to create a drug even more powerful than heroin. Anyone who thinks we can solve this problem without cutting off our wide-open border is either ignorant or lying.

How is it a fourteen-year-old girl in Delafield, Wisconsin, whose mother is a registered nurse and with no history of drug use in the family, gets hooked on Mexican heroin? I could ask the same about countless other young victims—just in Wisconsin—whose cases the former agent reeled off to me. Yet I know the answer: the news media is complicit in the disinformation campaign. Why aren't reporters calling and speaking to these Border Patrol officers, especially the retired ones, who are more than willing to talk, and getting to the bottom of the story? Probably because journalists would claim it is "racist" to suggest that our heroin problem is coming from Mexico.

My phone call with Dan Golvach, my visit to the border, and my discussions with law enforcement officials had rocked me to my core. I knew I needed more information. And I knew I needed to get this issue before the public.

I began speaking more to Maria Espinoza, who explained how Speaker Ryan had refused both to see her or answer her questions about the federal government's refusal to enforce immigration laws. So Maria suggested she pay a visit to Wisconsin and bring along some of the Angel Moms. Would I be an advocate on their behalf?

How can you say no? Why *would* someone say no?

I said YES!

Accompanying Maria was Michelle Root, whose daughter Sarah had been killed by a drunk street-racing illegal alien from Honduras; Agnes Gibboney, whose son, Ronald da Silva, was gunned down in his girlfriend's driveway by a previously deported illegal alien; Laura Wilkerson, whose son Josh was beaten, tied up, strangled, set on fire, and tortured to death by an illegal alien classmate Josh had offered a ride home from school. Dan's wife, Julie Golvach, would also make the trip to tell their story of their murdered son Spencer.

I listened to these women's stories, and I couldn't imagine how an elected official wouldn't immediately drop everything to do what he or she could for these brave Americans. It is nothing less than a civil servant's duty to prevent other citizens from becoming more statistics about illegal alien violence.

Of course, some will make the fallacious argument that "American citizens commit crimes too!" This misses the point. There should be zero crimes committed by illegal aliens in this country because there should be zero illegal aliens in this country. The crime rate comparison is a false equivalence. It's like saying it's illegitimate to discipline your child for being a messy eater in the school cafeteria because bears are also messy eaters in the school cafeteria. It's truly that ridiculous a comparison. An illegal alien has no more business being in this country than bears have being in your child's cafeteria.

At a time when so many of our citizens are suffering, illegals consume a tremendous amount of our taxpayer dollars. But what really infuriates me, even more than the waste, is the crime.

America is a rich nation. But that doesn't mean we have some sort of obligation to accommodate anyone who came here illegally, who overstayed his or her legal status whether on a visa overstay or for any other reason. The laws of this nation were designed to give *American* citizens freedom. They were not designed to benefit illegal aliens. That's what America First is all about.

In contrast, our elected leaders put America last. Indeed, they seem to regard American citizens as something akin to undesirable enemies who need to be replaced as quickly as possible. Democrats are quite clear about their intention to create an entirely new people and so enshrine a permanent progressive majority. Yet we also see Republicans like Speaker Ryan playing buddy-buddy with the likes of Luis Gutiérrez in order to give more benefits to illegals and enable more immigration. Meanwhile, he wouldn't even meet with the Angel Moms who had been hurt so badly by the policies he supports.

So we did the only thing we could. Outside the wall Ryan built around his mansion, with the Angel Moms in attendance, I called on Paul Ryan to tear down the wall around his home. If he didn't think America deserved protection from illegal alien violence, I saw no reason he should be allowed to protect his property.

The Angel Moms wore shirts emblazoned with the images of their slain children. They surrounded me in a semicircle as I called out Paul Ryan for his hypocrisy and his failure to fulfill his oath of office. Speaker Ryan happened to be home that day. When I was done speaking, the Angel Moms laid a quilt on the grass between the road and the sidewalk running parallel to the Ryan property. We took some photos and did not create the kind of disturbance you see when leftists protest at someone's house. We were respectful, not just because we weren't leftists, but because we were in a residential area and are just respectful by nature.

As we were walking back to our rally point at the local park, we saw something amazing. Ryan stepped out of the house. A few of the Angel Moms approached him with the intent of presenting him with a letter. Part of the letter read, "Speaker Ryan if you cared as much about our families as you do about your donors, our kids might still be alive today."

You know what he did next? He ignored them. He ignored them and hopped into one of the waiting SUVs to be whisked away to his next fund-raiser, leaving those women in the dust. I would never wish anything bad on the Ryan children or on his wife. But you have to ask yourself, if Paul Ryan had lost a child to illegal alien violence, is that how he would have wanted his wife to be treated if she had joined something like the Remembrance Project? As we made our way back to the park, I couldn't help but wonder what wounds Ryan had just reopened with his callousness.

As far as I was concerned, the gloves were off.

Those women would make another trip to Wisconsin's First District to campaign along with me and Ann Coulter in the final days of the campaign. The journalists, as you can probably guess, showed no interest in meeting with them or asking them about Paul Ryan.

As I said before, Ryan spends millions of dollars every two years in his campaign efforts. Who is going to bite the hand that feeds it? It's not as if journalists are expected to have any ethics.

But I bet if I had marched a half dozen "DREAMers" outside of Speaker Ryan's walled compound, demanding amnesty, I would have been swarmed by national media, with satellite trucks parked up and down the street, with journalists eager to write countless adoring puff pieces.

But why did the Angel Moms' message fall on deaf ears? How can people not react to the mother of a slain child working to prevent any further tragedies like the one that took her son or daughter?

The thing is, I don't think it did fall on deaf ears. I think the problem was that most Wisconsinites found it unbelievable that I had the audacity to blame Ryan, the favorite son, for his part in all of it. I heard many times we ran a race that was simply too blunt in its messaging for this part of the country.

The media was largely in Ryan's corner from the jump. He had an eighteen-year head start as a congressman and more years before that as a staffer. He answered softball questions because that's all he was thrown. You could count on a pleasant load of gibberish from Ryan every time he waved his "Better Way" agenda at the camera. Needless to say, he never turned any of these vague ideas into legislation. He just presented happy slogans. And the press let him get away with it.

I made every effort to smile and calmly assert facts that are indisputable. I tried to make the case that Americans are at risk for crimes by illegal aliens every day Paul Ryan is a congressman. My supporters in border states couldn't ask for more red meat than we gave them. These supporters donated and some even traveled across the country or made phone calls for me. But they couldn't vote.

Wisconsin is geographically far removed from the border.

When the dishonest media insists on referring to illegals as "DREAMers" and "the undocumented" and conceal facts about their illegal status in criminal cases, it's not surprising that messaging on immigration had a hard time breaking through. Besides, we raised $1.5 million to compete against an incumbent who *started* with a war chest of $4.5 million and eventually spent an unprecedented $10.6 million to retain his seat. That is ten times the average spent on a congressional race.

David and Goliath? It was more like David and Leviathan.

Unfortunately, the media had built a protective cordon around Paul Ryan, which made it difficult for me to challenge him not just on immigration, but on other issues.

For example, take the reauthorization of the Export-Import Bank (Ex-Im). Ryan had railed against Ex-Im just a few years before it finally lapsed. Here in Wisconsin's First Congressional district is Case New Holland, now a subsidiary of CNH Global NV, the holding company for the Italian public multinational manufacturer of agricultural and construction equipment.[8] This conglomerate was formed by an agreement between Shanghai Tractor, Internal Combustion Engine Corp., and Case New Holland's brand of agricultural equipment.

While "not all US exporters benefit from Export-Import Bank assistance, the ones that do often benefit handsomely," despite the fact that many of the firms "can arrange their own financing without the Bank's help."[9] So why does the American taxpayer need to fund $90 million of that multinational corporation's working capital or $270 million of their bank insurance?

Ryan was instrumental in Ex-Im's reauthorization.[10] The crafty thing is, he voted against it on the floor vote![11] When the leadership has the votes to pass something, they can vote against the same measure they took part in enabling. It's hypocrisy like this that Americans hate about politicians, especially when the politician in question, like Ryan, can't stop paying tribute to his own "principles."

Or, as another example, there was the time Ryan worked to engineer the PROMESA, the Puerto Rico Oversight, Management, and Economic Stability Act. I call it the Puerto Rico Hedge Fund Investor Bailout. Mark my words: in a few years there will be lawsuits from the bond investors who will be told that they have to take a "haircut" on their investments in Puerto Rico bonds. These bonds were junk to begin with, as Puerto Rico doesn't generate enough earnings to cover the bonds that they issue. Yet they were sold as good bonds by unscrupulous hedge fund managers. Prior court rulings on issues similar to this case (such as *United States v. Winstar Corp.*) suggest the United States government is open to a lawsuit when bondholders can claim the federal government shortchanged them. The inevitable settlement will be paid by the U.S. Treasury.

Logan Beirne, lecturer at Yale Law School said the PROMESA would basically allow bondholders to "front the money for the bailout while taxpayers would have to pay them back for this cash advance."[12] It smacks of cronyism, and we saw this in the past "when Congress changed the rules on investors in such a way that destroyed their property rights." The Supreme Court held the United States liable and required it "to pay more than $2 billion . . . in compensation to these investors." That's coming again.

Ryan didn't pen that legislation. He didn't vote for it. He escaped accountability for it. But you better believe he made sure the votes were there to get it passed. After all, it's not like the hedge fund managers didn't know the Puerto Rican bond crisis was going to hit.[13] And as Open Secrets shows, the majority of Speaker Ryan's campaign financing comes from inside the DC beltway from big banks, big law firms, and big insurance companies.[14] Of course he delivered for them.

Honestly, the blame doesn't just belong to Speaker Ryan. It belongs to the rest of the members of Congress who respond to each new "crisis" with bailouts to the politically connected.

But it was frustrating how Ryan personally was permitted to avoid being asked tough questions about his policies. He was never asked substantive questions about subjects such as the Trans-Pacific Partnership trade bill until he was finally forced to back away from it. Yet it was the free pass he was given on immigration that outraged me the most.

Think of how absurd it is that Speaker Paul Ryan, nominal leader of the GOP Congress, was the subject of a 2015 documentary showing how he worked with Luis Gutiérrez to secure amnesty. As Julia Hahn at Breitbart noted:

> While Ryan was "getting in bed" with Gutierrez to push amnesty, the whole affair had to be conducted in secret so as not to tip off Republican voters to their plan.
>
> "You feel like you have to kind of sneak around to have dinner with these guys," Gutierrez's communications director, Douglas Rivlin, said, referring to his secret meetings with House Republicans to push amnesty. "Unlike some of you [expletive deleted], I don't mess around with my wife, so—but let me tell you—right? I feel like I'm sneaking around right on my party . . . when I have dinner with you guys," he said.

Gutierrez confirmed, "Right. . . . We can't tell people. That's OK. Maybe that's the way this has got to get done. But if those are the rules, those are the rules."

The documentary explains that Gutierrez and Ryan's stealth amnesty operation hinged upon the secret support of House Freedom Caucus' founding member, Mick Mulvaney [R-SC].

"Here's the surprise," the narrator says. "The strategy is to target the hardcore Tea Party conservatives like Mick Mulvaney, guys who've even voted against Boehner in the speakership elections," a narrator explained. "If Tea Party stars support their bill, the more cautious Republicans will follow."

The documentary reveals how Mick Mulvaney is one of the most open borders members of the House.

At a Republican Party Breakfast in Goose Creek, South Carolina, Mulvaney demeaned his conservative constituents and colleagues, such as Steve King, who oppose Ryan's mass amnesty plan—suggesting that they are "absurd" and "stupid."

"We need to stop celebrating the absurd in our party and stop rewarding the outrageous and the stupid," Mulvaney declared as he made the case for disenfranchising his own voters with mass immigration.[15]

Ryan spoke to a group of illegal-alien DREAMers in Racine, Wisconsin, back on July 26, 2013. He was filmed saying, "If I was living in a country where I had no opportunity, where I was living in despair and poverty, and I was fearing for my safety and my family's well-being, I would go anywhere to make a better life for myself and my family. Who wouldn't do that?"[16]

Ryan then said we are a nation of laws. In the next breath, he essentially repudiated what he had just said by assuring attendees they were doing right by their children, implying they should stay here in the United States. Don't fix your country, illegally come wreck ours.

Can't make this stuff up, right? How are we not deporting illegal aliens who by definition are lawbreakers? How can we be a "nation of laws" when entire classes of people are magically exempt from the laws?

What it came down to was this: Ryan was perceived and portrayed as the Wisconsin nice boy. I was portrayed as deplorable. In fact, the local paper, the *Janesville Gazette*, vilified me for hosting the Angel Moms in front of Ryan's personal border wall with an editorial written by a board who refused to meet with me to get my side of the story.

How's that for fake news?

IMMIGRATION JIHAD

America's southern border is only one source of the national security risk created by our government's dereliction of duty. What's even more shocking is our government's determination to import new national security threats. I refer, of course, to our so-called refugee resettlement program.

Even the name is a lie. "Refugees," under international law, are supposed to be those fearful of being persecuted because of their race, religion, nationality, or membership in a particular group. Yet President Barack Obama admitted very few Christian refugees, even as Middle Eastern Christian communities that had existed for millennia were practically wiped out because of Islamic extremists enabled by our suicidal foreign policies. Instead, he gave massive amounts of funding to transporting Sunni Muslims into our country, though that is the very group doing the persecuting.

Who are these refugees? Do we even know? Well, vetting of these so-called refugees is handled by the United Nations, an organization that has shown hostility toward our national interests. The pools the UN draws from are predominantly resettlement camps. Christians and others are summarily persecuted if they try to take refuge in a resettlement camp. The UN High Commissioner for Refugees (UNHCR) also works closely with the Organization of Islamic Cooperation (OIC). The OIC is an international Islamist group of fifty-seven Muslim nations whose founding charter seeks to propagate jihad and sharia, or, law based on the Quran. That explains why 99 percent of the "refugees" entering the United States are Muslim.[17]

It is not even up for debate that we cannot vet these people. The FBI has openly admitted it is impossible.[18] So why deliberately do this? How does this possibly serve our national interests? And who benefits from it?

Of course, Muslim groups in the United States may support this because they want to add to their numbers and their electoral clout. Leftists support it because the more Third Worlders they can import into our country, the more votes they can expect to get. Corporations may support it because they see a new source of cheap labor. But the easiest group to identify are those who participate in what I call the refugee resettlement business.

There's big money in dumping migrants on unsuspecting American communities. The U.S. government works through groups it has designated as VOLAGs (voluntary organizations). That is a catchy term to give you the impression that we're dealing with a bunch of good-hearted souls that exist to help people. Actually, it's because they profit from it.

Well over a billion dollars is spent each year for refugee resettlement, *not* including the welfare benefits and government services given to these people.[19] Much of that money goes to "charities," many of which are ostensibly Christian or Jewish. These "nonprofits" receive money from the federal government, but do not have any responsibility for the migrants they impose on the country. Indeed, after a few months they are not even required to know where the migrants live. Groups such as the Catholic Church have even cut traditional charity efforts to increase involvement in the refugee resettlement racket.[20]

I'm every bit as pro–free market as your typical Trump supporter, but this is insane. And it's not capitalism. It's a government welfare program writ large. What we have here is a system designed to pay people to bring in refugees. And what is truly despicable about this is those who use guilt or appeal to compassion to argue for bringing more "refugees" are really just acting in defense of their own personal profit. It's the most immoral scam imaginable.

What is truly contemptible is how many of these "Christian" or "Jewish" organizations seem utterly indifferent to defending the lives of Middle Eastern Christians, the people who actually are being hunted down like dogs in their ancient homelands. Those who claim to profess belief in Christ don't want to defend their brothers and sisters in the faith unless they can make a buck off of it. And we are supposed to look to these people for moral leadership? It is time this racket be exposed for what it is, an organized criminal syndicate whereby our own government subsidizes treason.

Who is brought into this country by these so-called

Christians and Jews? Overwhelmingly, Muslims. I'm going to dispense with the happy talk about Islam being a religion of peace. The word *Islam* directly translates to "submission," not "peace." The news media has gotten away with that sleight of grammatical hand for too many years now.[21]

Political correctness is dead. If you fall for it, it may get you killed. You choose. *Islam* means "submission." And an Islamic America is no longer America.

Let's examine what the Quran actually says. It's important to remember that the Quran, unlike the Bible, is described as the literal words of God, not something inspired by God (2 Timothy 3:16) or open to interpretation.[22] What you see is what you get.

The foundational texts of Islam forbid Muslims from integrating into our society. That's the bottom line. I can quote chapter and verse from the Quran, because like Thomas Jefferson, I've read it. I've also read the Sunnah (the accounts of the Islamic prophet Muhammad's daily practice) and many of the hadiths as well. On top of that I've read in-depth analysis of the Islamic faith written by former U.S. intelligence officers and watched hundreds, maybe thousands of hours of lectures and films distributed by Islamic imams.

It is true that there are "moderate Muslims." But there is no moderate Islam. Moderate Muslims are simply not obeying the dictates their faith imposes upon them. So it doesn't matter to me that you know a nice Muslim or that you have read otherwise; it is right there in their texts.

Therefore, we should not expect a reformation of Islam to occur except in the direction of stricter adherence to the word of their god. And that's really the point of groups such as ISIS and the Muslim Brotherhood. They interpret Islam directly, accurately, from the foundational texts of the faith.

What is one of the things they are told in these texts? It is hijrah—migration in the name of Allah, Islam's deity. Why? To force all people of all faiths to submit or face the sword. Mass migration is a weapon of war.

What do they want everyone to submit to? Sharia law. Sharia is a religious system of law mandated by Islam which enforces draconian punishments and discriminatory treatments between men and women. Leaving Islam is a crime; apostasy is punished by death. Christians must live as *dhimmis,* second-class citizens subject to a special tax. Homosexuals are subject to the death penalty in countries governed by this system including Iran and Saudi Arabia. Women are not considered equal to men when it comes to giving testimony in court. Sharia also allows men to beat their wives. This is the system that so-called progressives, even feminists and LGBT activists, seem so determined to defend.

Philip Haney, former analyst at the Department of Homeland Security and the author of *See Something, Say Nothing,* explained:

> The power that drives the global Islamic movement isn't actually jihad. It is the goal to implement global Sharia law. Jihad is the tactic that is employed via various kaleidoscopic forms by the different groups that are all seeking the same thing.
>
> The type we're most familiar with is jihad by the sword, but it is by no means the only form of jihad. People who are Muhajirun, people who immigrate to a foreign country for the sake of implementing Islam, receive the same reward in heaven as those who fight with the gun. It's an implicit understanding. They know from the time they were children,

if they immigrate, if they became Muhajirun, they are guaranteed the same reward as the Mujahedeen, the ones who fight with guns.[23]

If we know that the Islamic religion contains a sizable population that believes in sharia over secular law, and even in sharia over the U.S. Constitution, why are we risking our freedom by permitting a hijrah designed to conquer and replace us?

During my work on the documentary *Hijrah: Radical Islam's Global Invasion*, I often saw attempts to explain away this concept. You may encounter someone who tells you that hijrah doesn't mean to migrate somewhere, but just to "leave sin behind." The word does indeed have two meanings. Imams will teach both meanings, but for the mainstream media, they only share the more peaceful, spiritual meaning.

Yet what does the Quran say?

Fighting is prescribed for you & ye dislike it. But it is possible that ye dislike a thing which is good for you & that ye love a thing which is bad for you. But Allah knows & ye know not. (Quran 2:216)

Fight those who believe not in Allah nor the Last Day, nor hold that forbidden which hath been forbidden by Allah and His Messenger, nor acknowledge the religion of Truth, (even if they're) of the People of the Book [Christians], until they pay the Jizya [tax] with willing submission & feel themselves subdued. (Quran 9:29)

Let those fight in the cause of Allah Who sell the life of this world for the hereafter. To him who fighteth in the cause of Allah—whether he is slain or gets victory—Soon shall We give him a reward of great (value). (Quran 4.74)

Or consider one of the hadiths, known as Sahih al-Bukhari."

The Prophet said, "The person who participates in (Holy battles) in Allah's cause and nothing compels him to do so except belief in Allah and His Apostles, will be recompensed by Allah either with a reward, or booty (if he survives) or will be admitted to Paradise (if he is killed in the battle as a martyr). Had I not found it difficult for my followers, then I would not remain behind any Sariya going for Jihad and I would have loved to be martyred in Allah's cause and then made alive, and then martyred and then made alive, and then again martyred in His cause."[24]

I always find it surprising how few Christians have actually read the Quran. Jesus is a character in the Quran. I say "character" because there are many names from the Bible in the Quran, including Adam and Eve, Noah, Abraham, Moses, and Mary, the mother of Jesus. But the narrative is fundamentally changed. Indeed, Christians and Jews are insulted in the Quran, and Muslims are enjoined not to make friends with them:

O you who believe! do not take the Jews and the Christians for friends; they are friends of each other; and whoever amongst you takes them for a friend, then surely he is one of them; surely Allah does not guide the unjust people. (Quran 5:51)

The Quran even makes a reference to Christians and Jews being incarnated as "apes and pigs."[25]

Unlike what Christians believe, Muslims believe they have to earn their way into heaven; they are not accepted on faith.

And war is one of the ways to earn their way in. According to chapter 47 of the "Book on Government" of the Sahih Muslim, a collection of hadiths considered legitimate by Sunni Muslims, "The Messenger of Allaah said 'One who died but did not fight in the way of Allah nor did he express any desire (or determination) for Jihad died the death of a hypocrite.'"[26]

In other words, die during the performance of jihad and you are automatically granted a place in heaven.

The words of the texts are clear. And again, unlike in Christianity, the core text, the Quran, is the *literal* perfect word of God, not subject to interpretation. If Muslims want to practice their faith separate from sharia, that's up to them. The world could be a much more peaceful place if that were the case. But that is not what the Quran tells them to do. And that is certainly not the example their "prophet," Muhammad, set for them.

Sharia is the problem. Political Islam is the mechanism by which it works to undermine any society in the Dar al-Harb, the "House of War"—all countries outside the control of Islam. The end goal is for the entire world to become the Dar al-Islam, the House or Abode of Islam, where all "infidels" (including Christians and Jews) will be subjugated. The intent is for sharia law to govern everything.

Why should we be forced to submit to this? Why should we implement any policies that make this outcome likely in any corner of the West? And why are our leaders, who are supposed to represent *us,* after all, so eager to defend and even propagate Islam? I'm not the first to notice how the leftists who spit on believing Christians adopt the most radical Muslims almost as a kind of mascot.

In the long run, the country is not just a geographic

expression, a piece of magic dirt. The country is the nation, the people. And if the nation is replaced by a new Islamic population, the country will become an Islamic country, governed by sharia. Refugee resettlement furthers this process, especially when our leaders seem to go out of their way to deny that mass Muslim immigration will irrevocably transform our country.

Indeed, our leaders don't seem to know anything about this faith that they are inviting into our midst. All they can offer are banal platitudes that show they haven't even considered the issue.

Paul Ryan, in condemning then candidate Trump's "Muslim ban," had cooed, "The vast, vast majority of Muslims in this country and around the world are moderate. They're peaceful. They're tolerant. And so they're among our best allies, among our best resources in this fight against radical Islamic terrorism."[27]

George Bush famously said after the September 11 terrorist attacks, "The face of terror is not the true faith of Islam. That's not what Islam is all about. Islam is peace. These terrorists don't represent peace. They represent evil and war."[28]

Even Pope Francis absurdly claims, "Authentic Islam and the proper reading of the Quran are opposed to every form of violence."[29]

But none of this is true. Even a casual reading of the Quran shows it is not true. And it is simply insane to suggest that moving vast numbers of Muslims into our country won't have any negative effects.

Elected officials have a duty and a responsibility to secure the existence of America and a future that does not subjugate our children to Islam. When leaders like Paul Ryan fail to live up to their sacred oath of office, every American is less safe.

In my race against Paul Ryan, I railed against the basic safety considerations ignored when it came to refugee resettlement. We had national security agencies in clear language stating that the vetting process was broken. There were even Muslims admitted into our country who had previously been arrested on terrorism charges overseas.[30]

Even the Obama administration banned immigration from Iraq for a time and identified seven nations in the "Terrorist Prevention Act of 2015" as problematic countries who deserved extra scrutiny when it came to admitting their nationals.[31] Upon taking office, President Trump signed an executive order establishing a temporary halt on the same seven countries Obama had chosen for scrutiny. The hysterical treatment Trump received from the mainstream news media compared to Obama has been eye-opening.

Unfortunately, it seems leading Republicans are too often willing to join in these disingenuous media campaigns. During the presidential race, then candidate Trump said that he would enact a temporary Muslim ban in order to ensure the safety of American citizens in the face of a clearly broken vetting process. The mainstream news media were apoplectic. And so was Paul Ryan. The Speaker wasted no time signaling to journalists that he would sue Donald Trump if he enacted a Muslim ban.[32]

It gets worse. Speaker Ryan funded every dangerous refugee resettlement program, immigration amnesty, and sanctuary city in the country.[33]

I waged the battle for America because somebody has to put the security of American citizens first. It sure wasn't going to be Barack Obama, Paul Ryan, or anyone else in the Democrat or GOP leadership. It might as well be me.

4

TRADE WARS

JOHN GODFREY SAXE FAMOUSLY SAID, "Laws, like sausages, cease to inspire respect in proportion as we know how they are made."[1] (It's usually misattributed to Bismarck.) What we hear from the politicians and the mainstream media about certain laws is usually the opposite of what they actually do. It's as if they have completely disconnected words from their meanings.

Here's an example: free trade.

What free trade means to the normie (normal, everyday

person who watches the mainstream media and believes *that* is the truth) is that there are no tariffs or restrictions on trade. It's supposed to liberalize trade policy. But what if I tell you that a particular trade deal has all sorts of complicated regulations designed to benefit large corporations or particular donor groups, not the broad swath of American businesses and consumers?

Well, that doesn't sound free. It doesn't sound fair. It sounds like just another scam.

Well, in a nutshell, that's what you have with the Trans-Pacific Partnership.

Besides, why would we want a fair shake anyway? Who the hell wants a level playing field? This is ludicrous if you think about it. We should want the playing field tilted in our favor!

American workers have been getting shafted by bad trade deals for decades now. Don't you think it's time we wage the battle for the American people and defend our own collective interests?

That's what an America First trade policy looks and feels like. You should *expect* to have several jobs to choose from. You should *expect* your salary to increase by 10 percent every year. It has in China for the last ten years, most years over 10 percent per year.[2]

I've got your attention now. I know it. It's exciting to think you will have several jobs to choose from and that your salary will increase a lot year after year. It should. Americans are the most innovative workers in the world. This is coming from someone who has managed workers all over the world, so I'm not just blowing smoke at you. Americans are the best, hands down!

But we can't do that until we reform our trade policy. Let's start by looking at what TPP was all about.

The way I'm going to explain this very complex trade deal

to you is by giving you a broad overview of how the deal came together, who was in on it, and how it was foisted upon the American public and sold to us as a free trade deal. Furthermore, I'm going to walk you through the triggering events that took this trade deal down to the 5-yard line. I'm then, in subsequent chapters, going to break down several of the most egregious aspects of the "free trade deal," because killing TPP was not the end.

Mark my words. Congressional leaders beholden to their corporate donors are going to try to bring something like this back in another form. And we need to be able to rebut it point by point.

This is a story of deceit that would make Benedict Arnold blush. If I can get you to grasp the magnitude of how bad this was, you will never look the same way at a "free trader" again. My hope is that the phrase is retired to the dustbin of history.

We dodged a bullet on this deal, one aimed at workers' wages in virtually every industry. I can't think of an industry that this trade deal wouldn't have negatively impacted in some way. It was that close to a touchdown for the globalists and the multinational corporations that treat humans like interchangeable widgets, or, worse, like pawns in their diabolical global chess game that puts America's workers in checkmate.

THE BROAD OVERVIEW

The TPP was designed as a twelve-nation trade deal. The United States, Australia, Brunei, Canada, Chile, Japan, Malaysia, Mexico, New Zealand, Peru, Singapore, and Vietnam were the signatories to the initial deal. I say "initial" because there was a provision for more countries to join the TPP after it was signed by the largest economy—*ours*.

We fully expected China to join the TPP after it was ratified, along with a slew of Muslim nations. I'll get back to that and why it's important in just a bit. To give you some perspective on the relative sizes of the gross domestic product (GDP)—think of that as the economic output of a nation—of the countries involved in the TPP, please refer to the following table:

TPP PARTNER RELATIVE GDP

PARTICIPANT	TPP GDP % TOTAL
UNITED STATES	66.18
JAPAN	16.87
CANADA	5.46
AUSTRALIA	4.48
MEXICO	3.79
SINGAPORE	1.06
CHILE	0.84
PERU	0.64
NEW ZEALAND	0.64
BRUNEI	0.04

You can see that the GDP of the countries is *yugely* different. You might also notice that the combined total of the eleven smaller countries do not equal the GDP of the United States. It isn't even close! This "free trade deal" was marketed as encompassing 40 percent of the trade of the entire globe. But take the United States out of that calculation and the number drops to 15 percent of the global GDP output.

Now consider this: the populations of the countries involved dwarf the population of the United States. Let's think about that for a moment.

At the most basic level, if you are trading with those who have a much larger population but a much smaller GDP than you, there is going to be a serious imbalance. It means that most of those you are trading with are not going to be able to afford any of the goods that you want to sell. Japan, a relatively high-wage, low-population nation, already has its market satisfied by Japanese manufactures. The lower-wage nations, meanwhile, can't afford American goods. Therefore, America will be buying the products of the foreign nations in the trade deal, but those nations will not be buying from us. Instead, the poor countries will be contributing the only thing they can contribute: labor. And Japan will gain access to the vast American market, while America essentially gets nothing in return.[3]

The dirty little secret that nobody wanted to let out was that there were chapters in the trade deal, specifically chapters 10 and 12, that allowed for increased legal immigration. That's what this deal was designed to enable. Cheap labor for American corporations, access to the American market for foreign corporations, and pink slips for American workers.

THE NUTS AND BOLTS

Now, the negotiations for this trade deal were conducted for over half a decade. Back in Obama's first term, Hillary Clinton was deeply involved in the TPP. While secretary of state, Hillary Clinton called it the "gold standard" for international trade agreements, something she blatantly lied about during the presidential debates.[4]

"Gold standard." What a bucket of hogwash. It was a train wreck for America. The Japanese were the next biggest economy in the trade deal, and their economy is dwarfed by the size of the U.S. economy. And they were by far the country with the highest average income and largest economy. Brunei, Vietnam, and Malaysia have little to contribute except cheap goods and cheap labor. And we are already stuck in NAFTA with Canada and Mexico.

We can see how TPP would have played out by looking at the trade deal we did with South Korea back in 2011 known as KORUS. KORUS has been a huge success—for South Korea. In just over five years they have managed to double the trade imbalance with the United States, with the effect of us losing about a hundred thousand jobs.[5] Seriously, you could hardly find anything good to say about the KORUS trade deal unless you are heavily invested in South Korean factories.

How did the Obama administration manage to screw up a bilateral trade deal? Simple. We had the wrong people at the table. The South Koreans had respected business leaders who are nationalists. They put South Korea First. The Obama administration put America last. So the interests of small and midsized American manufacturers and the vast majority of workers weren't even considered.

We have to consider what is the point of trade policy. I believe it is to open up markets to our goods and increase revenue for our companies, with the ultimate purpose of benefiting American workers. But for those who run our country, it seems that the purpose is to increase revenue to foreigners, flood our own market with cheap foreign goods, and drive our own workers out of the labor market. That's what happened with KORUS. And the TPP would have been much worse.

TRUMP, TRADE, NATIONALISM

For the office of United States trade representative, President Trump selected one Robert Lighthizer, a man who served Ronald Reagan as deputy U.S. trade representative. Lighthizer, who has persistently fought in the private sector against trade deals that would disadvantage Americans, once said of Senator John McCain: "'Mr. McCain may be a conservative. But his unbridled free-trade policies don't help make that case,' suggesting that free trade had long been popular among liberals."[6]

It reminds me of this riff that candidate Trump would use on the campaign trail when he was working the crowd into a fervor: "And we will win, and you will win, and we will keep on winning, and eventually you will say we can't take all of this winning . . . please Mr. Trump . . . and I will say, NO, we will win, and we will keep on winning.'"[7]

This is precisely the mind-set we need when it comes to trade. It's a competition. Our nation is competing against other nations. And the purpose of our government is to defend the interests of our companies and workers. Donald Trump seems to understand this on a gut level, as does Lighthizer. And as you'll see, that's something that those who put together the TPP never got.

BACK TO THE NUTS AND BOLTS

Obviously, if the welfare of the American nation is not your primary concern, you want to hide that from the voters. So, just as with Obamacare, the Obama administration negotiated the deal in secret.[8] After it was kept secret for quite some time, they let some select elected officials see it. Not all of them. And those who saw it couldn't take any pictures of it and couldn't sneak out any notes related to it. They essentially had to memorize it.

Why would you do something like this unless you were trying to get something over on your constituents?

Of course, there was a way around the news blockade. I went to the New Zealand website and looked at New Zealand's copy of it. Seriously, they were reporting in the mainstream media that it was in a locked bunker while I was on the computer reading it and marking it up. It wasn't available on the United States Trade Representative website (ustr.gov), but I had my own copy.

Our news media is so gullible and lazy they don't even try anymore. It really angers me, to be honest. This was almost the end of the United States of America. We might have well been called the United States of Asia had this trade deal gone through.

After the trade deal went past a certain point in negotiations, the American people were told that it was necessary to be put on a "fast track." Fast track authority simply means that Congress cedes its authority to amend or filibuster trade deals. Amazingly, Speaker Ryan and Majority Leader Mitch McConnell were leading this effort to give Congress's authority to President Obama. The only reason you would do this is because you don't want to allow the possibility of political opposition against the trade deal.

Why would there be opposition? As mentioned before, Speaker Ryan eventually opposed TPP. But he never mentioned that TPP relinquishes American sovereignty to unelected foreign bureaucrats when it comes to determining a global trade structure which will have massive effects on American workers and companies. Speaker Ryan claims TPP needs to be renegotiated. Really it just needs to be ended.

But that doesn't mean I oppose trade. In a speech at a local tool manufacturer in Racine the Monday before the primary, Ryan disingenuously made the case for trade deals, saying the United States needs to engage on the world stage. He insinuated that those opposed to TPP do NOT want trade. Nothing could be further from the truth.

We *do* need trade. But we need bilateral trade deals. We need to flex America's muscle when we negotiate a trade deal. The only way to do that is one-on-one. That's what bilateral means. And it means America's vote is equal to the vote of the country we're dealing with, as opposed to something like TPP, where each nation gets a vote on certain issues. See how much more powerful we are with only one other trading partner?

When Ryan was specifically asked about the Trans-Pacific Partnership by a worker, he criticized the deal, saying it needs to be renegotiated, and that the votes aren't there to pass it. There's just one problem with Speaker Ryan's conversion on TPP: Speaker Ryan is to blame for preventing Congress from going back to the drawing board to fix TPP!

Under our Constitution, it is Congress that has the power to make laws. Paul Ryan sought to give away that power when he gave Barack Obama the so-called fast track, or trade promotion authority (TPA). TPA greases the skids for TPP, and handed the reins for the trade deal over to Obama. Congress can no longer amend any trade once the president has TPA. As a result, Congress is limited to an up or down vote on the entire deal. If anything, this dramatically reduces the odds of getting a good trade deal. If there is a specific flaw in a deal, Congress would have to reject the whole thing in order to stop it. It's worth noting that NAFTA was also passed through fast track.

But Ryan continued to misrepresent what TPA means. He claims that TPA gave the United States trade representative "the ability to go negotiate trade agreements."[9]

That is a bald-faced lie.

After all, the USTR has been negotiating the TPP for more than half a decade by now, and only got trade promotion authority in June 2015.

All trade promotion authority really does is tie Congress's hands so that it can no longer ask the trade representative to go back and renegotiate certain sections. It's Congress ceding its own responsibility to make laws and caving to the imperial presidency.[10] Paul Ryan whipped the votes in Congress to pass trade promotion authority while claiming that the USTR would follow Congress's instructions.

In fact, Speaker Ryan wanted to ensure that the only edits that could be made to TPP would be made by President Obama or a future President Hillary Clinton. Speaker Ryan's entire characterization of how TPA and TPP work together is a globalist fairy tale.[11]

TPA erased Congress's "constitutional role" in the trade deal by giving it over to President Obama. Congress is tasked in Article I, Section 8 with regulating commerce between the United States and foreign nations. Congress must also approve treaties, the obvious expectation being that they would have a say in the actual text of the treaties. Fast track trade promotion authority is a way around those little constitutional formalities.

Once President Barack Obama had the authority, he used it. On August 12, 2016, he issued a document that set in motion a minimum thirty-day wait before he could present the legislation that would have committed America to the TPP. He also said the treaty would not change any federal, state, or local laws to comply with the trade deal.[12]

This is not true. TPP would have forced local and state laws to be harmonized with the treaty.[13] This trade deal would have brought unlimited foreign workers to replace Americans in our jobs here at home. It would have been a deal made with countries that essentially use slave labor and who do not protect their workers. It was a deal made with countries that do not have the same environmental protections or food standards that we have in America.

It was NAFTA on steroids. And Hillary Clinton, Barack Obama, and Speaker Ryan pushed TPP because they value globalism over America.

WHY THIS IS SO PERSONAL

When you've been so fortunate to lead more than ten thousand employees in companies all around the world, you start to feel a real empathy for your workers, even a sense of responsibility. You have a personal stake in those employees' well-being, and you want good things to happen to them even after you move on to another business. It's as painful to hear of layoffs of former employees as it is gratifying to hear of their promotions.

What's completely unacceptable is to hear your own Congress pushing for a trade deal that puts all their careers at risk.

I fought this trade deal on behalf of every American who wants a secure job, a safe America, and a future that doesn't relegate them to an existence of serfdom driven by global elites. And I did it because I thought of the workers I used to lead.

Never did it occur to me to run for office—not until months

after Paul Ryan decided to push for fast track trade promotion authority for President Obama's (and Hillary Clinton's) Trans-Pacific Partnership trade deal. Even then, I thought someone would emerge as a challenger to the right of Ryan.

I would simply volunteer to help get that person elected.

But no one emerged.

The Trans-Pacific Partnership was bad on so many fronts that I said on more than one occasion I would have run on this issue alone. The reality was that Paul Ryan was the champion of this trade deal before he was Speaker of the House. His ascension to that position made the issue paramount. In the absence of someone challenging Ryan, I'd have to do it.

And that was calculus that led me to the decision to run against one of the most powerful elected officials in the United States.

This trade deal risks the welfare and sovereignty of Americans.

Paul Ryan is the champion of this deal.

He lives in my district.

Nobody else is stepping forward.

I must do this.

There wasn't anything else that entered the equation.

I told my wife I was prepared to do this, and we discussed it, but at no point was it a negotiation. I'm sure she would have been happier if I had stayed in business and stayed out of the public eye. That said, she's a warrior and supported the cause.

Before I formally announced my candidacy, I sought out my dear friends Jay and Julia. I've known them since 2008. They are retired but not over the hill. When I floated the idea to them, their response was "We love you, dear, and you'd be great, but you will get beat up doing this. Wait until the next cycle."

But I couldn't. TPP was on the brink. I had to fight it right *then*. I had to beat it right then. It was my duty to wage the battle.

So, I did my research. Prepared as I'd prepared many times before for many business situations. You can't prepare for everything, but you can get a good handle on one issue and dissect it so that you can kill it when the time comes.

As I said before, that's just what my campaign did.

Now let's talk about why that was so important. And why Americans need to still be on guard.

AMERICA'S TRADITION OF ECONOMIC NATIONALISM

"FREE TRADE" IS SOMETHING AKIN TO HOLY WRIT within the Republican establishment. Both Donald Trump and I were heavily criticized for even questioning it, as if we had committed some kind of blasphemy. Some of Trump's critics on the right refused to concede Trump's contention that free trade was incompatible with nationalism. As Ben Shapiro wrote in the *National Review* before the election: "Those of us who champion free trade do so not out of an altruistic desire to enrich people abroad, but because free trade has made America the most powerful economic force in human history."[1]

But is that really true? The history of the United States, and the history of the Republican Party, suggests there is a strong America First tradition when it comes to trade. Indeed, one could argue this country was not built by free trade, but by an economic policy that emphasized domestic manufacturing, high wages for workers, and investments in infrastructure. Donald Trump's campaign was simply the latest manifestation of the traditional American economic policy. Such policies go back to the founding of the republic itself.

Today, absurdly, Alexander Hamilton is best known to many Americans (and undoubtedly, most journalists) as the subject of a hip-hop musical on Broadway. But Hamilton was the man who laid the foundation for America's future economic prosperity. Though usually presented as being "pro-British" and a champion of the Eastern merchants, Hamilton expressed a virile nationalism and a determination for our young country to break away from British economic, as well as political control. Indeed, he drew a connection between the two.

For example, he wrote in his famous Report on Manufactures, "Not only the wealth; but the independence and security of a Country, appear to be materially connected with the prosperity of manufactures. Every nation, with a view to those great objects, ought to endeavour to possess within itself all the essentials of national supply. These comprise the means of Subsistence habitation clothing and defence."[2]

Hamilton, as well as the other Founding Fathers, understood independence meant little if the new United States was simply going to be an economic colony of the banks in London.

The only way to avoid this fate was for America to build up its own manufacturing capability and increase its domestic markets. One of the very first things the federal government ever did once it began operating under our present Constitution was to pass the Tariff Act of 1789.

The "American System" under figures such as Senator Henry Clay was also an important part of our early national history. This included a protective tariff designed to build up American industries as well as building infrastructure, such as railroads. This kind of a system was also seen as a way to avoid class conflict by giving everyone in the country common economic interests. Henry C. Carey defended this kind of a system in his book *The Harmony of Interests*. Carey, one of the nation's most influential political economists, would write several letters detailing his proposed policies to our nation's first Republican president: Abraham Lincoln.

Lincoln, too, supported relatively high tariffs and the development of American infrastructure. He was "one of the most ardent protectionists in American politics during the first half of the nineteenth century."[3] The Morrill Tariff of 1861 introduced a policy that would largely stay in place until the Wilson presidency. It was under this kind of economic policy, which emphasized putting American industries first, that the United States became the leading economic power of the world. These tariffs were also how our government paid for its operations during these years of economic expansion.

When the tariffs were massively reduced, the government introduced a new policy to pay the bills: the income tax. I find it hard to argue that the move to the income tax was somehow a triumph for "limited government."

The idea that conservatives are somehow stalwart defenders of "free trade" is nothing less than a rewriting of history. But don't take my word for it. Ask Robert Lighthizer.

In 2011, Lighthizer wrote:

> For most of its 157-year history, the Republican Party has been the party of building domestic industry by using trade policy to promote U.S. exports and fend off unfairly traded imports. American conservatives have had that view for even longer.
>
> At the beginning of this nation, Alexander Hamilton and his followers were staunch conservatives who helped found American capitalism—and avowed protectionists . . . During the first half of the 19th century, pro-business politicians like Henry Clay were ardent supporters of an "American system" that would use tariffs to promote American industry. Clay's political descendants—such as Abraham Lincoln—went on to form the Republican Party. Every Republican president starting with Lincoln—and for almost 100 years thereafter—generally supported tariffs, while Democrats tended to promote free trade.[4]

As Lighthizer pointed out, more recent Republican presidents also used tariffs. I'll use my favorite example. I'm a motorcycle enthusiast. My Harley-Davidson is one of my most prized possessions (and something I loved to use even in campaign ads). And in 1983, in an action specifically designed to protect the Harley-Davidson Motor Company of Milwaukee, President Ronald Reagan introduced tariffs that raised the rates on imported heavyweight motorcycles.[5]

Will these same people who constantly denounced

Donald Trump tell us that even Ronald Reagan wasn't a "true conservative"?

America wasn't built by free trade. It was built by the American system of developmental capitalism, which puts American workers, manufacturers, and products first. That's the kind of tradition I want to return to. I don't think American politicians should be forcing us in a global race to the bottom. Our workers should not have to compete with everyone in Asia in a contest of who can survive on the lowest possible salary.

Yet that's what TPP was designed to do. Unfortunately, it seems as though that's what a lot of recent trade deals have been designed to do. And much of this was enabled by Congress giving away its authority to negotiate trade deals to the president.

While the United States has always participated in international trade, it wasn't until 1934 that Congress granted the executive branch the ability to negotiate bilateral trade agreements with the passing of the Reciprocal Trade Agreement Act (RTTA), and separately, but alongside it, the Export-Import Bank.[6] President Roosevelt would create two banks to facilitate trade: one with the Soviet Union and the second with Cuba. They were combined in 1935 through an act of Congress.

Fast-forward to 1947, when the RTAA was abrogated by the General Agreement on Tariffs and Trade (GATT). The GATT was then replaced with the World Trade Organization in 1994. What was happening was a gradual process of the United States surrendering its control over tariffs to international bodies and institutions.

During this same time frame, average tariff rates the United States imposed on other countries fell from a high of 44.6 percent in 1870, to 15.6 percent in 1934, to 5.5 percent in 1948, to 2.6 percent in 1995, to 1.3 percent in 2010.[7] Without going into huge detail, you can see the general historical trend from a large protective tariff to essentially a nonexistent one.

As I mentioned, not quite a hundred years ago was the first time Congress gave the executive branch the ability to negotiate bilateral trade deals. That's a trade deal between the United States and one other nation. One of the deals thus negotiated would pave the way for the notorious North American Free Trade Agreement (NAFTA.). This was the Canada–United States Automotive Products Agreement. It was also known as the Auto Pact, or APTA.

APTA removed tariffs on cars, trucks, buses, tires, and automotive parts between the two countries. This deal was passed in 1965 and was fifty-five pages long, including the president's message, background information, and analysis.[8] APTA essentially consolidated two national auto manufacturing industries into one. It effectively locked foreign manufactures (European and Asian) out of the Canadian market and locked in American automakers.

Canada would disproportionately benefit from the deal in the long run. The Canadian plants built smaller cars. During the price shocks of the 1970s, created by the oil shortages, the Canadian facilities expanded production on a per-unit basis at a rate higher than the American facilities.[9] Generally, as with most trade deals, there was a mixed reaction. Yet we can probably say Canada and the United States both benefitted inasmuch as thousands of jobs were created in Canada. More total cars were produced on both sides of the border throughout most of the agreement. Struggles on the American side had more to do with the rising oil prices than with this deal.

APTA was abrogated in 1987 by the passage of the Canada–United States Free Trade Agreement, not to be confused with NAFTA.[10] This new agreement was 315 pages long and covered a much broader scope of products and services, including technical standards, agriculture, wine and spirits, energy, automotive, government procurement, services, investment, temporary entry for business persons, financial services, institutional provisions, and other provisions, such as intellectual property. It can be reasonably compared directly with NAFTA in scope.

Another trade deal that was a precursor to NAFTA was the United States–Israel Free Trade Agreement, passed in 1985. The U.S.–Israel FTA was the first such free trade agreement entered into by the United States.[11] That agreement is about 13 pages long, plus additional explanatory material.

There are a few interesting characteristics to this agreement. While it is claimed there exists no tariff with the exception of agricultural products, Israel imposes a series of taxes and fees on all imported products sold in their country: 1 percent on the cost, insurance, and freight (CIF) of the goods, a 0.5 percent stevedoring fee, a purchase tax on luxury and certain consumer items, and a value-added tax (VAT) of 17 percent.[12] There is no corresponding reciprocal penalty for Israeli products shipped into the United States. This is hardly a "free" trade agreement, but simply a deal that biases one side over the other.

Still, even though the deal is biased against us, it has a logical way of settling disputes. This trade agreement covers all products and services traded between the two nations. If there is a disagreement, there is a procedure whereby the two nations work it out. If they cannot reach agreement, the dispute progresses to a joint committee. If there is still no agreement, it proceeds to a three-person conciliation panel, with each side selecting one member and those two members selecting the third member to act as chair. The panel makes a finding of fact and presents its findings. The report of the panel is nonbinding.

This mechanism may seem clunky, but notice how it doesn't directly infringe on American sovereignty. Remember this procedure—because what was proposed in TPP was something vastly different.

This brings us to NAFTA, the North American Free Trade Agreement, signed by President Bill Clinton on December 8, 1993. It's more than 1,700 pages long: 741 pages for the treaty itself, 348 pages for annexes, and 619 pages for footnotes and explanations. It is difficult to see how 1,700 pages of government rules and regulations translates to free trade. By definition, free trade is the removal of government from the trading process, not its expansion.[13] Compare the length of NAFTA to the length of prior agreements and the scope of government intrusion in the markets is glaringly apparent.

Contrary to past trade deals, NAFTA set up a separate "Free Trade Commission" and a secretariat. An unelected bureaucracy that would interpret and, crucially, impose decisions is quite a departure from the trade deals of the past. It is anathema to the proper function of the American republic. Indeed, it denies national sovereignty altogether. Why would we grant foreign nationals the ability to foist decisions upon our corporations, jurisdictions, and citizens?

One part of the treaty, known as Chapter 11, gives investors the right to sue foreign governments without having to pursue court actions in that country's court system. In theory, it prevents foreign investors from "discrimination." In practice, it means foreign investors have a way to get around domestic laws. Originally, this provision was designed to protect against corruption in Mexican courts. But the country being sued the most is Canada.[14] It's just another example of how these kinds of deals always have unintended consequences.

The most recent trade deal, which we've touched on before, is America's agreement with South Korea, referred to as KORUS. This trade deal went into effect in 2011 and is seen as the prototype for the Trans-Pacific Partnership. Surely you've heard all the great things about KORUS touted on TV and all of the jobs created in America as a result of this trade deal, right?

No?

Hmm. Why do you suppose you haven't heard glowing endorsements for KORUS? You guessed it. It has been a disaster. Between 2011 and 2015, the trade deficit with South Korea has doubled, and not in America's favor.

We've lost another one hundred thousand jobs to a small country like South Korea through this trade deal. Bilateral trade deals are the best trade deals, but the Obama administration even managed to screw that one up.

Yet even KORUS was nothing compared to what would have been inflicted on us if TPP had passed. Let's look at the specifics.

6

THE WAR ON SOVEREIGNTY

THE OFFICE OF THE UNITED STATES TRADE REPRESENTATIVE
now hosts the full text of the TPP agreement.[1] The preamble
claims the agreement will promote "economic integration to
liberalise trade and investment, bring economic growth and
social benefits, create new opportunities for workers and businesses, contribute to raising living standards, benefit consumers,
reduce poverty and promote sustainable growth."[2]

I would argue that TPP would have crushed social benefits

and living standards, taken away opportunities for American workers, benefited only the wealthy elite, and increased poverty. But there is so much more harm this agreement would have done.

We need to go through this because this is what your elected leaders intended for you. It would have turned America into nothing but an outpost of a larger United States of Asia. It also tells you something about the priorities of President Obama, Hillary Clinton, and Michael Frohman, who was the United States trade representative responsible for overseeing the negotiations of the Trans-Pacific Partnership. And it tells us something about the media, who refused to cover what this trade agreement would have done and allowed Paul Ryan to get away with not debating me on it.

There were so many problems with TPP, it's hard to know where to begin. But let's start with the most fundamental point. As with NAFTA, TPP frankly denied American sovereignty, creating a new international organization with the power to impose regulations on the United States. But don't take my word for it. Look at the treaty itself. And start with chapter 27, the seven articles of which set up a body with more authority than Congress to decide issues that will affect the lives of millions of Americans.

THE WAR ON SOVEREIGNTY
Article 27.1 reads:

> The Parties hereby establish a Trans-Pacific Partnership Commission, composed of government representatives of each Party at the level of Ministers or senior officials. Each Party shall be responsible for the composition of its delegation.[3]

This is a body superior to Congress. Congress will have no say, contrary to what you've been told in the media, except through the one unelected bureaucrat who votes on behalf of the entire United States of America.

That's right: one vote. Each country will get one vote, just like the five permanent members of the UN Security Council. Except in this case it will be one in twelve.

That is a weak vote. Why did we settle for a weak hand in this deal? Since it is a majority vote to make changes to the treaty, the United States will be at a huge disadvantage to small nations.

Consider how our power will be limited compared to a weak nation like Brunei, for example. This small country on the island of Borneo is home to just over four hundred thousand people and a GDP of $16 billion (less than Vermont's). And they would have a vote equal to America's on things such as what rules the countries have to adhere to in production.

Since the TPP includes Indonesia, which has the largest Muslim population in the world, and other Muslim countries, it could even mean a push for sharia compliance for member nations.

Another troubling aspect is that "the Commission and all subsidiary bodies established under this Agreement" will make decisions by "consensus," unless provided otherwise (art. 27.3.1). It goes on to say in the footnotes that any decisions about alternative decision making shall itself be taken by consensus. That's not reassuring. Consensus means that the eleven other TPP countries can vote against the United States on every decision. Naturally, they would do that to strengthen their hand against ours. Call it an America Last policy.

Who will head this commission? Well, according to the

treaty, meetings of the Commission shall be chaired successively by each party, which is to say, each nation. Some of the countries participating in TPP have horrible human rights records. American workers would be competing with Vietnam, Malaysia, and Brunei, all of which have documented human rights violations, including slave labor. Yet those countries will be the ones in charge.

Unacceptable.

The next chapter of the treaty, chapter 28, similarly denies American sovereignty. It's also a massive break with precedent in how our government used to handle trade disputes. I thought the US–Israel trade deal was too biased against America, but at least when it came to trade disputes, American independence was respected.

Recall: If there was a disagreement, there was a procedure whereby the two nations work it out. If they can't, the dispute progresses to a joint committee. The last step if there is still no agreement is a three-person conciliation panel, each side selecting one member and those two members selecting the third member to act as chair. The panel makes a finding of fact and presents its findings. The report of the panel shall be nonbinding.

Everyone can understand that. And that it is nonbinding means that if a country feels that it is operating in the interests of its country, it may continue to do so. At least in theory, under this kind of a system, America could put America first and Israel could put Israel first. And that's entirely natural and moral. What's more, in most cases there will be an agreement. You don't break deals if you can find any kind of solution. So, having a "nonbinding" way out is important because any issues that do arise are likely to be very serious.

TPP doesn't work that way. Not by a long shot. Article 28.3.1(c) says a party has a legitimate dispute when a "benefit it could reasonably have expected to accrue to it" under trade agreements is "nullified or impaired as a result of the application of a measure of another Party that is not inconsistent with this Agreement."[4] What this means is that foreign companies would have a grievance against the United States if our laws and regulations prevented them from making a profit. And of course, these laws and regulations include those things that ensure our food is safe and that products that are being sold are not dangerous. Under TPP, America essentially loses even the right to enforce this legislation.

Let's take an example. If a country wanted to sell bad shrimp to us and we prevented it, under TPP America would be forced to pay for tainted food it returned to the offending partnering nation. Sound absurd? America has already received tainted food shipments from nations included in the TPP agreement.

According to Bloomberg, "The FDA inspects food shipments to the United States, including seafood shipments, but the agency's resources are limited . . . It is able to inspect fewer than 3 percent of shipments. Of that . . . , much is sent back. The FDA has rejected 1,380 shipments of Vietnamese seafood since 2007, finding filth and salmonella.[5]

If TPP were in force, the companies who tried to market this filth would have a way to sue *us*. You might object that they would just lose in court. Ah, but they won't be suing through the American court system. Consider how chapter 11 of NAFTA has provided a way for companies to sue the Canadian government. Now, in TPP, article 28.3.1 states that "dispute settlement provisions of this Chapter shall apply . . . when a

Party considers that a benefit it could reasonably have expected to accrue to it is being nullified or impaired as a result of the application of a measure of another Party that is not inconsistent with this Agreement."

Didn't get the market access you wanted? File a dispute.

Didn't make the profits you expected? File a dispute.

Can you imagine trying to defend yourself or your business or your local/state government in this scenario? Ludicrous.

But it gets worse. Where will the forum even be? According to another part of chapter 28, "The complaining Party may select the forum in which to settle the dispute" (art. 28.4.1).

What's to stop an "aggrieved party" in Brunei, with their strict sharia penal codes, from raising a complaint against a Christian business in the United States and holding the forum in Brunei?

Not one thing. What's the Christian business's recourse? Zilch.

In the United States, case law has been built up over the course of more than two centuries. It is that case law that makes the U.S. legal system so attractive to foreign businesses who want to do business in the United States. Businesses do not like uncertainty. Markets do not like uncertainty. Casting aside legal precedent and established case law in favor of kangaroo courts and secret tribunals would further weaken American jurisprudence.

In disputes, again, there will be a three-person panel. Under a complicated procedure, far more detailed than that in the U.S.–Israel Free Trade Agreement, a third person to the panel is ultimately selected after one is chosen by each side. But what if the two sides can't agree on the third person? That "Commission" established in article 27.1 ultimately makes the choice.

Think the commission will choose a panelist who will be neutral to the proceedings?

I wouldn't bet America's national independence on it.

All this sounds Byzantine, but it would impact the rights of any business owner who does any kind of trade with any of these nations. Since, ultimately, the commission chooses the third panelist in a body that decides disputes, and since TPP makes it almost impossible for an American to be chair of a panel adjudicating a dispute where an American is involved (unless both sides agree, which would never happen), your rights and property will be subject to the whim of foreigners. What's more, if the panel is unable to reach consensus, that commission decides by "majority vote." Congress, of course, is never consulted.

TPP also introduces a way for left-wing activists or radical environmentalists to inject themselves into the proceedings. According to article 28.14, a party that isn't a disputing party but "considers it has an interest in the matter before the panel" must simply send a written notice and then be entitled to attend hearings and make presentations. The next section provides for panels to "seek information and technical advice from any person or body that it deems appropriate" (art. 28.15)—in other words, "experts."[6]

What kinds of well-funded groups do you think will be closely monitoring these disputes and seeking to influence the process? I'd bet none of these third parties have the interests of the American worker at stake. This simply enables a parade of far-left NGOs (nongovernmental organizations) to insert themselves into business disputes.

As any businessperson will tell you, one of the worst things you can do to investor confidence is introduce instability. What TPP does is provide a complicated way for foreign competitors or meddling activists to interfere with American businesses. What's more, American businesspeople will have no real way to fight back. This introduces an element of chaos and doubt in every contract, negotiation, or agreement conducted internationally. After all, thanks to TPP, any party at any time could simply invent a dispute and kick the entire matter over to one of these unelected tribunals.

In a truly Orwellian note, when a decision is made, article 28.18.2 says no panel will ever "disclose which panelists are associated with majority or minority opinions." So, you don't even get to know who is on this secret tribunal that has power over your business. Furthermore, the treaty says, "No Party shall provide for a right of action under its law" (art. 28.22), meaning that this secret tribunal's rulings essentially become more powerful than our own Constitution!

Did our Founding Fathers risk their lives, fortunes, and sacred honor for TPP? What would even be the point of national independence?

THE SCOPE OF TPP

A jealous defense of American sovereignty does not mean opposition to international trade. America has always traded with the rest of the world. But we have the largest economy in the world in nominal terms and the second-largest economy in the world according to purchasing power parity. Put bluntly, we offer more to the vast majority of potential trading partners than what they offer us. This gives us leverage, which is best used in bilateral trade deals. Not using this leverage is nothing less than a betrayal by our elected officials to guard the national interest of our country. As I'm sure President Trump might put it, deal from strength or get crushed every time.

As mentioned before, the Obama administration managed to screw up the KORUS bilateral trade agreement. But that was a failure of that team's negotiating ability, not of the larger principle. We want to maximize leverage by keeping trade deals as controllable as possible, not by creating sprawling, chaotic agreements that out of necessity must be moderated by international institutions hostile to American interests.

Unfortunately, TPP, like NAFTA, was another one of these agreements that grew out of control. It didn't just cover trade per se. It covered topics such as intellectual property, cross-border trade in services, temporary entry for business persons, and administrative and institutional provisions. It also imposed a vast regulatory framework on American corporations.

Many of these areas, under our Constitution, are under the purview of Congress. Indeed, even our own government already overregulates American companies, creating huge economic distortions and hurting our economy. Yet TPP would have made matters even worse by handing control of these areas over to international organizations already against us.

When I worked all over the world running various businesses, I always loved returning to the United States and hearing "Welcome home" uttered by every customs officer as you cross back into American territory. There's a palpable sense that you are coming back to a place that is *yours*, a place where you have real control over your life. That simply would not have been the case if President Trump had not been elected and killed TPP.

The scale of the treaty ensures these organizations would have a huge amount of control over our laws.

One of the most devastating sections was chapter 20, "Environment." What this section of the treaty did was institutionalize many of President Obama's climate change initiatives. It's a great mystery why a Republican Congress, put into office by voters who overwhelmingly reject this scam, allowed TPP to go forward, and even gave President Obama more power to implement it.

One of the sections of TPP (Article 20.3.7) claims that nothing in the treaty can be construed as empowering one country's authorities to intervene in the territory of another country in order to enforce immigration rules.[7] But this actually provides a huge loophole. After all, it's not that Chile, for example, intervenes in the United States to enforce environmental laws. There are larger international organizations. And the rules that are to be enforced will be determined, as we've already seen, by secret tribunals that override American law.

Section 20.3.5 says each party has the right to exercise "discretion" "with respect to other environmental laws determined to have higher priorities." Notice how this vague reference to "other environmental laws" is not a reference to the laws each country makes for itself. It opens the door for TPP's tribunals to enforce international environmental agreements. This is especially ominous when one considers how the United Nations, under its Agenda 21 plan, is surreptitiously imposing outrageously invasive land use plans in local communities around this country.[8]

This is explicitly recognized in Article 20.4.1. It says the parties "recognise that multilateral environmental agreements to which they are party play an important role, globally and domestically, in protecting the environment—accordingly, each Party affirms its commitment to implement the multilateral environmental agreements to which it is a party." Later, TPP commits signatories to address "energy efficiency; development of cost-effective, low emissions technologies and alternative, clean and renewable energy sources; sustainable transport and sustainable urban infrastructure development; addressing deforestation and forest degradation; emissions monitoring; market and nonmarket mechanisms; [and] low emissions," as part of the "transition to a low emissions economy" (art. 20.15.2).

Again, here we have an international institution setting policy priorities for the American government. It's also obvious this is a backdoor way to insert Agenda 21 into American communities. In 2012, the Republican National Committee called Agenda 21 "a comprehensive plan of extreme environmentalism, social engineering, and global political control." So why didn't they oppose TPP directly?[9]

This section would have had a massive impact on American workers and consumers, as it would have enabled the destruction of the American fracking industry. Despite President Obama's best efforts to sabotage it, fracking has thrived and has become a major support of our economy[10]

According to a 2016 report by Colin Chilcoat, a specialist in Eurasian energy affairs and political institutions:

> U.S. crude oil production is up more than 85 percent, or some 4.5 million barrels per day since 2008, after years of steady decline; dry natural gas production rose more than 25 percent in that time. . . .

The shale boom created jobs; and it did so at a rate nearly 40-times greater than that of total private sector employment from 2007 to 2013. The full unconventional value chain is estimated to support over 2 million jobs and more than $150 billion in earnings. Further, residential, commercial, industrial, and electric power customers saw gains of approximately $74 billion combined in the aforementioned period. Adding in oil—and the resultant drop in gasoline prices—IHS estimates that households save roughly $2,000 annually due to unconventional production.[11]

Yet TPP seems designed to sabotage this critical economic pillar of our country's prosperity. According to article 20.12.9 of TPP, one party can request a "dialogue" with another party if "an environmental law at the sub-central level of government of the first Party is not being effectively enforced by the relevant sub-central government." This is of course aimed squarely at American states and localities. As it stands now, the Environmental Protection Agency (EPA) is notoriously hard-handed with the states and contemptuous of their rights. But now, other nations will have a way to crack down on American states who have policies foreign nations can claim are hurting their investments.

The worst part of all of this? We get to pay for our foreign competitors! It says in the United States Trade Representative's overview of the "free trade deal" that "some of TPP's lower-income members may require support to strengthen the scientific and regulatory agencies that administer and enforce these laws."[12]

Translation: American taxpayers, the "higher income" members of this treaty, will have to subsidize the lower income members. Ridiculous.

Article 20.17.7 also says signatory nations will be "creating and participating in law enforcement networks," essentially forming a kind of global police. Is that what we want? Do we really want to create law enforcement networks with Islamic countries that enforce strict sharia enforcement codes? In what alternate universe does that even seem marginally reasonable? Certainly, there's nothing in the United States Constitution that says we should be doing anything like this.

Had we passed TPP, it would have meant the end of American sovereignty. And the danger is not past. Like a zombie, the globalist message is never truly put down. It keeps coming back for more. And that's why we must look to what they tried to do in the past to guard against their efforts in the future.

THE WAR ON AMERICAN WORKERS

IT'S NOT JUST THAT TPP STRIPPED AMERICA of the ability to make our own laws. It also prevented us from controlling who enters our country.

One of the biggest controversies of the recent election was whether TPP essentially forced the United States to have de facto open borders. Senator Jeff Sessions, now President Trump's attorney general, alleged that TPP gave the Obama administration unilateral authority to expand immigration.

Paul Ryan, naturally, dismissed this as an "urban legend." Bob Goodlatte, who heads the House Judiciary Committee, denied TPP was an "immigration giveaway."[1]

But what did TPP actually say?

According to article 10.5, "no Party shall adopt or maintain . . . measures that impose limitations on . . . the total number of natural persons that may be employed in a particular service sector or that a service supplier may employ and who are necessary for, and directly related to, the supply of a specific service in the form of numerical quotas or the requirement of an economic needs test."[2]

As Rosemary Jenks, director of government relations for Numbers USA, confirmed, TPP increases the number of L-1 visas and tourist visas that can be used for business purposes. TPP is not technically changing immigration law in this regard, but only because the number of both of these visas is unlimited. Article 10 holds that any service provider can now enter into the United States and provide that service. The obvious result is that every company will admit an unlimited number of cheap foreign workers to provide services. And thanks to TPP, there will be no legal way to stop them.[3]

What's more, article 10.6 states unequivocally that a foreign business will not be compelled to have an office in the United States as a condition for doing business here. Thus, contrary to the lies of those who said these types of agreements would bring jobs to America, it would do nothing of the sort.

Consider how this would play out. Say we decided to start a business in Vietnam to supply Vietnamese agricultural workers across the United States. As a shared service, those workers will migrate north and south in the United States as the growing season ebbs and flows. Those workers will be housed in communal-type arrangements that will be leased by the company. The workers will be paid the minimum wage afforded Vietnamese workers, which is currently about $0.64 an hour. They will be driven to and from their worksites and provided meals and work uniforms.

If this sounds like a prison work crew to you, you're not alone! It sounds an awful lot like indentured servitude to me. Didn't we fight a war over that in this country?

We are going to incorporate the business in Vietnam, and we will hire local Vietnamese recruiters to supply us with labor resources from the labor pool in Vietnam. But who will actually run the company? That's right: a consortium of American agribusinesses.

An agreement like this essentially allows companies to capture an entire low-cost labor pool. It's both a cheap labor handout and a nuclear bomb directed at our immigration laws. And it wouldn't just apply to agriculture. It would apply to every industry you can name.

Furthermore, according to the agreement, licensing procedures can't be used as "a restriction on the supply of the service." Additionally, according to article 10.9.4, "a Party shall not accord recognition in a manner that would constitute a means of discrimination . . . in the application of its standards or criteria for the authorisation, licensing or certification of service suppliers, or a disguised restriction on trade in services."

Of course, discrimination is the basis for awarding degrees and certifications. You don't just waltz into the university provost office and demand a degree. It is conferred once you earn it. Discrimination is good and effective that way.

Once this is abolished, the American market will be flooded with unqualified (but cheap) workers. We won't need to argue over H-1B or H-2B or any classification of workers at this point. They will be sent here and we would have to deal with it. Period.

Coincidentally, not long after I announced my candidacy for Wisconsin's First Congressional District seat, Michelle Malkin, John Miano, and Sara Blackwell visited with Abbott Labs employees just south of the Wisconsin border. Those workers had recently lost their American IT department jobs to less skilled foreigners from India on H-1B and other guest worker visas.[4]

Michelle, John, and Sara are tireless fighters for American workers. They advocate for reducing worker visas and putting our own people first.

Because after all, the jobs didn't go away. That's the mind-bending part of all this. The jobs are still in Illinois. The American workers were told that they had to train their less-skilled replacements before they could collect their severance checks. Jeb Bush was a supporter of the program. Marco Rubio was a supporter of the program. Paul Ryan is a supporter of the program. And TPP would have made even this system seem like nothing.

TPP is still important because it is a preview of what the globalists ultimately want. Even skilled workers would be replaced by cheap foreign labor. For that reason, I campaigned hard against H1-B visas.

Of course, I also had to deal with "fake news" coverage because of this opposition. A local radio personality and Never Trump activist named Charlie Sykes told his listeners that I had worked for a company that used the visa waiver program. Had

Mr. Sykes had the foggiest idea of how a corporation operates, or bothered to ask me if I had ever had anything to do with the utilization of visa waiver programs, he would have found out that I was never involved with bringing foreign workers to the United States to replace Americans. Sykes and his listeners would also have learned that I had instead brought work back to the United States from Canada, Mexico, and China, creating American jobs and making more money for American companies.

Besides, by Sykes's argument, the remaining workers at Abbott Labs at all levels of the organization would be somehow tainted because the CEO replaced some of their colleagues with foreigners. There's a twisted bit of logic to get your head around.

It's important for all Americans to pay close attention to this because every profession is at risk. For example, annex 10-A of the TPP agreement deals specifically with professional services. Think professional engineers, architects, and lawyers. Annex 10-A.2 calls for "recognising professional qualifications, and facilitating licensing or registration procedures." Other sections similarly call for procedures to "promote the mutual recognition of professional competence in engineering and architecture, and the professional mobility of these professions" (10-A.5).

As an engineer, this is especially personal to me. American professional engineering qualifications are built on a foundation that has been reinforced with time and experience. This strict and exceptionally rigorous qualification and regulation scheme began in 1907 in Wyoming. We have durable buildings, bridges, and other man-made structures that are a testament to the standards maintained and continually upgraded through the process of obtaining and maintaining (through continuing education) a professional engineer's license in all states in America.

Yet look at how the TPP's authors view it. The language about "recognising" members of professions like engineering in the countries of Brunei, Chile, Mexico, and Vietnam is just plain wrong and dangerous. By the "harmonisation" of standards (art. 10.9), what they really mean is abolishing standards. Professional engineering needs to be strictly regulated and have the highest demands for competence and knowledge. Instead, TPP is a way to hollow out this profession as well as so many others, and replace America's skilled workers with unqualified cheap labor.

The cost won't just be shoddy workmanship and a collapse in professionalism. When it comes to designing buildings and infrastructure, lives will be at stake.

A similar procedure is urged for lawyers. The agreement calls for making it easier for "transnational legal services." As part of that, according to annex 10-A.10(c), "local ethical, conduct and disciplinary standards are applied to foreign lawyers in a manner that is no more burdensome for foreign lawyers than the requirements imposed on domestic (host country) lawyers."

This means foreign lawyers would only be held to the standards of Third World nations and would still be able to operate here.

Three words. *Foreign. Ambulance. Chasers.* What could possibly go wrong?

I'm betting the American legal profession was not fully briefed on this "free trade deal." While we've been discussing trade and focusing on trade disputes, this section would validate foreign attorneys undercutting American attorneys' wages in all manner of cases.

Indeed, you could even imagine banner ads for foreign

attorneys competing with American attorneys driving down the cost of American legal services. It's a gut buster, right? I'm guessing all the law schools in America wouldn't have been laughing when enrollment in foreign law schools skyrockets. Had TPP passed, American students would start taking Internet-based classes to obtain their foreign law degrees, which would have been recognized in American courtrooms based on the slick maneuvering that got this trade deal fast tracked in the first place.

They told us this trade deal wasn't a back door to immigration. Really it was something worse. It was a full-scale lowering of the drawbridge.

When the news media reports on trade deals, they focus on the impact on blue collar workers. But we can't do that anymore. Every job was at risk with this so-called free trade deal. It didn't level the playing field. It simply made Americans second-class citizens in their own country.

Besides, as stated earlier, we shouldn't want a level playing field! We should want our own government to do everything it can to put our own citizens first.

Instead, there was one other section to this treaty that made it perfectly clear Americans weren't just to be subjugated but replaced. According to article 12.2.3 of the TPP agreement, nations were allowed to prevent entry of other people, but only "provided that those measures are not applied in a manner as to nullify or impair the benefits accruing to any Party under this Chapter."[5]

And there you have it. If it would harm the trade interests of one of the TPP members, you cannot apply border controls. Besides, if there is any dispute over what this section means, it will be the very nations pushing for more immigration who will be interpreting this clause and who get to decide it.

Indeed, there are some disturbing parts of this treaty that seem to suggest immigration restrictions need to be reduced as soon as possible. Article 12.3.1 says each nation must answer "as expeditiously as possible after receipt of a completed application for an immigration formality." Why is the speed at which an immigration bureaucracy operates the subject of an international treaty?

Annex 12-A demands each nation "specify the conditions and limitations for entry and temporary stay, including length of stay" for the temporary entry of business persons. That's a decision for our own lawmakers. What business is that of other nations?

Article 12.8.b demands that "programmes and technology related to border security" be shared, including "those related to the use of biometric technology, advanced passenger information systems, frequent passenger programmes and security in travel documents."

That's an eye-opener. Why would we agree to divulge our border security measures? This is beyond the pale. We have Islamic terrorists clamoring to get into America, and here, written into a massive trade deal, is a key demanding access to our lock.

TPP wasn't so much a trade deal as a battering ram designed to break down our restrictions on immigration. And these specific provisions and articles are important to track because the globalists will surely try to bring this back, either in a later agreement or piecemeal. They know they can't win an electoral battle by running on explicit open borders. So they tried to sneak it in.

But just because TPP was defeated doesn't mean the threat is gone. Patriots need to be on guard—and be aware of the enemy's text. Remember TPP, because even though they'll call it something else, it will assuredly come back.

8

THE WAR ON INTELLECTUAL PROPERTY

IT WAS THE MIDDLE OF THE AFTERNOON and I had just gotten off the phone with an irate customer. Our delivery for a high-capacity aquatic water filter was past due, and the customer was up against a hard deadline for opening a water park. Not good. I checked with my factory crew and found that the item that was holding up the shipment was located in a long queue. I immediately went to the sales team to see if we could sneak it up ahead of less-critical shipments with later install dates. After some phone calls and e-mails, we managed to squeak the order out on time without negatively impacting other customers.

That's usually how it goes in business. Except that this particular component was continually a problem. While I hadn't been with this team for very long, I'd encountered the problem before. After spending a couple of hours in the machine shop and then out in assembly, I had a brainstorm: maybe we could make a change to the part that would substantially decrease the time it took to make the final product. I pulled the electronic blueprints up on the computer, sketched some concepts in my notebook, and then made the notations on the computer.

The changes meant we'd have to reach out to a supplier who had some equipment we needed. We'd also need some prototypes built. I called a supplier we were using for similar work on another product line and discussed it with him. We got approval to get the prototype going; I'd have parts shipped from Wisconsin to Rhode Island a few weeks after the special tools were cobbled together and there was a production slot to drop them in.

Not bad for an afternoon of work.

Later that evening, it struck me: not only would this method change save us over 70 percent of the time to produce the part; it would give us capabilities that the current part didn't offer. That's huge. Suddenly we were talking about a patentable idea to a filter whose origins began more than a hundred years ago in America's early machine and sheet metal fabrication plants.

It was about 8 p.m. and I still hadn't eaten dinner, so I went back to my apartment and ate, then began poring over the United States Patent and Trademark Office's website, searching for devices similar to the one I'd thought up earlier in the day.

I was encouraged to find there were none with quite the same characteristics.

My first item of business the next morning was to see if we had a patent attorney on retainer. When I found we did, I called and spoke with him about what might be coming down the pike. He suggested I send over the sketches and the investigative work I'd done the night before.

Patentable or not, it would significantly reduce our problem with the lead time of product should the prototypes work out as I had hoped they would. We'd go down two tracks at once: improve the product lead time, and work on securing the intellectual property with a patent. The attorney later told me it wasn't quite patentable unless I did some more work to describe the differences between what I had made and what already existed.

It took me a good thirty to forty hours poring over the documents and referencing the USPTO portal to check and double-check what looked like a real opportunity. We decided to pursue it. I wrote up, to the best of my ability, a description of the device, and after some back-and-forth with the attorney, we felt we had a good submission. We filed for the patent on October 14, 2014.

While working on something completely unrelated a few days later, I saw how some of the same concepts could be used in a different industry, this time heat exchange. Since we had done considerable research on the fundamentals with the first submission, this submission was put forward and filed on November 7, 2014.

Now the fun began. Our first submission was rejected in the first quarter of 2015. We resubmitted it with slightly clarified verbiage. The second submission came back with mixed messaging, some good results and some parts rejected in total. The resubmission process can take the form of simply refiling paperwork or of a formal meeting with the examiner. I was fortunate to have David M. Driscoll as my patent attorney, and even more so to have him meeting with the examiner.

The process was arduous, but we were ultimately successful with both submissions, with two different examiners on two different inventions.

David and I would work together on several more brainstorms over the course of about twelve months to achieve patents on six more inventions in the United States and three international patents, with others still in process. I'm very fortunate God blessed me with parents who were smart and inquisitive, and encouraged the same in their children. I'm very thankful for that, and for the fact that I get to ply my trade as a citizen of the United States.

This process plays itself out across the United States and around the world on a daily basis for countless individuals with a good idea and a great attorney. We are fortunate that the framers of the United States Constitution knew one of the essential elements to making America great was the protection of intellectual property.

Article I, Section 8 of the Constitution says that Congress has the duty "to promote the Progress of Science and useful Arts, by securing for limited Times to Authors and Inventors the exclusive Right to their respective Writings and Discoveries." The Constitution could not be more explicit on this critical issue.

But even this fundamental bedrock of American prosperity is under attack. According to chapter 18 of the Trans-Pacific

Partnership agreement, "The protection and enforcement of intellectual property rights should contribute to the promotion of technological innovation and to the transfer and dissemination of technology, *to the mutual advantage* of producers and users of technological knowledge and in a manner conducive to social and economic welfare, *and to a balance of rights and obligations.*"[1]

Did you read in Article I, Section 8 of our Constitution anything related to balancing rights and obligations or mutual advantage? No, because it's not there. The Framers built a system in which individuals could build wealth and further technological progress. But here, TPP views scientific progress from the standpoint of the global collective.

Indeed article 18.13 says nations "shall"—not "may"—cooperate through "coordination, training and exchange of information between the respective intellectual property offices." Naturally, this will not be to Americans' advantage. This would turn the U.S. Patent and Trademark Office into an institution that will actually facilitate the theft of intellectual property by foreign nations. Remember the secret tribunals from article 28? How better to dethrone America as the world's innovators than to co-opt her USPTO into something different from what it is today?

The USPTO is unmatched and the envy of countries worldwide. It doesn't require fixing by the rest of the world. Yet another section of the treaty calls for different nations to "reduce differences in the procedures and processes of their respective patent offices" (art. 18.14.3). Article 18.40 even calls for "limited exceptions to the exclusive rights conferred by a patent, provided that such exceptions do not unreasonably conflict with a normal exploitation of the patent and do not unreasonably prejudice the legitimate interests of the patent owner, taking account of the legitimate interests of third parties."

With a United States patent, the patent holder alone decides how and to whom to grant access to his or her IP (intellectual property). The patent holder may choose to exploit the invention for his or her own gain, lease the IP to an interested party, or refuse to let anyone else use it.

If implemented, the TPP, or anything similar to it, will strip American inventers of their exclusive right to make that determination.

Let's say you come up with an invention to improve the gas mileage of automobiles by installing your contraption instead of the air filter on the car. You receive a patent and lease the technology to all the auto manufacturers. Soon you're making a good bit of money on the deal.

A few years into the patent, you see a mother with her infant and you have another brainstorm. Your auto device—the critical, intellectual part of it—could also improve the incubators used in hospitals so that babies born prematurely would get better air for them to survive.

You look on the USPTO website, which has now been co-opted by the forces of globalization through the TPP "free trade deal" and discover to your amazement that there is a Japanese company using your technology in just the way you had intended to use it. They aren't paying you to lease the technology, so you file a lawsuit—which winds up in article 28 proceedings, thanks to the architects of TPP. You lose the lawsuit because the tribunal determines that this limited exemption was granted for the good of humanity.

The fact remains that this *foreign* company is selling *your* technology—your intellectual property—and is making a profit off of it. They are also selling it for 1,100 percent of the cost that you would have sold it, because you would not have priced the device out of the reach of any clinic or hospital. That company doesn't have your sensibilities, but they have your intellectual property. And the reason they have it is because American trade negotiators gave your rights away.

Indeed, article 18.44.1 calls for pending patent applications to be published eighteen months from the filing date. Of course, patents take time to issue for many reasons. I should know, as I've been blessed to obtain seven U.S. patents and several foreign patents.

TRANSACTION HISTORY: US PATENT 9,127,896[2]

DATE	TRANSACTION DESCRIPTION
07-18-2016	ENTITY STATUS SET TO UNDISCOUNTED
	(INITIAL DEFAULT SETTING OR STATUS CHANGE)
06-13-2016	CORRESPONDENCE ADDRESS CHANGE
09-08-2015	RECORDATION OF PATENT GRANT MAILED
09-08-2015	APPLICATION READY FOR PDX ACCESS
	BY PARTICIPATING FOREIGN OFFICES
08-20-2015	E-MAIL NOTIFICATION
08-19-2015	ISSUE NOTIFICATION MAILED
09-08-2015	PATENT ISSUE DATE USED IN PTA CALCULATION
08-13-2015	DISPATCH TO FDC
08-13-2015	DISPATCH TO FDC
08-13-2015	APPLICATION IS CONSIDERED READY FOR ISSUE
07-01-2015	ISSUE FEE PAYMENT VERIFIED

DATE	TRANSACTION DESCRIPTION
07-01-2015	ISSUE FEE PAYMENT RECEIVED
06-05-2015	E-MAIL NOTIFICATION
06-05-2015	MAILING CORRECTED NOTICE OF ALLOWABILITY
06-02-2015	CORRECTED NOTICE OF ALLOWABILITY
06-01-2015	ELECTRONIC REVIEW
06-01-2015	E-MAIL NOTIFICATION
06-01-2015	MAIL NOTICE OF ALLOWANCE
05-26-2015	NOTICE OF ALLOWANCE DATA VERIFICATION COMPLETED
05-12-2015	INTERVIEW SUMMARY—APPLICANT INITIATED—TELEPHONIC
05-12-2015	INTERVIEW SUMMARY—APPLICANT INITIATED
05-15-2015	DATE FORWARDED TO EXAMINER
05-14-2015	RESPONSE AFTER NON-FINAL ACTION
04-15-2015	ELECTRONIC REVIEW
04-15-2015	E-MAIL NOTIFICATION
04-15-2015	MAIL NON-FINAL REJECTION
04-09-2015	NON-FINAL REJECTION
04-08-2015	CASE DOCKETED TO EXAMINER IN GAU
04-07-2015	CASE DOCKETED TO EXAMINER IN GAU
04-06-2015	INFORMATION DISCLOSURE STATEMENT CONSIDERED
03-30-2015	CLOSE TI
03-30-2015	CASE DOCKETED TO EXAMINER IN GAU
03-30-2015	TRANSFER INQUIRY TO GAU
03-04-2015	TRACK 1 ON
03-04-2015	DATE FORWARDED TO EXAMINER
03-02-2015	RESPONSE TO ELECTION / RESTRICTION FILED
02-10-2015	ELECTRONIC REVIEW

DATE	TRANSACTION DESCRIPTION
02-10-2015	E-MAIL NOTIFICATION
02-10-2015	MAIL RESTRICTION REQUIREMENT
02-05-2015	RESTRICTION/ELECTION REQUIREMENT
02-05-2015	CASE DOCKETED TO EXAMINER IN GAU
01-23-2015	E-MAIL NOTIFICATION
01-20-2015	MAIL-RECORD PETITION DECISION OF GRANTED TO MAKE SPECIAL
01-16-2015	RECORD PETITION DECISION OF GRANTED TO MAKE SPECIAL
11-07-2014	ELECTRONIC INFORMATION DISCLOSURE STATEMENT
12-01-2014	APPLICATION DISPATCHED FROM OIPE
11-24-2014	E-MAIL NOTIFICATION
11-21-2014	SENT TO CLASSIFICATION CONTRACTOR
11-21-2014	FITF SET TO YES—REVISE INITIAL SETTING
11-07-2014	PATENT TERM ADJUSTMENT—READY FOR EXAMINATION
11-24-2014	APPLICATION IS NOW COMPLETE
11-24-2014	FILING RECEIPT
11-07-2014	PGPUBS NONPUB REQUEST
11-20-2014	APPLICANT HAS FILED A VERIFIED STATEMENT OF SMALL ENTITY STATUS IN COMPLIANCE WITH 37 CFR 1.27
11-07-2014	TRACK 1 REQUEST
11-07-2014	PETITION ENTERED
11-11-2014	CLEARED BY OIPE CSR
11-07-2014	INFORMATION DISCLOSURE STATEMENT (IDS) FILED
11-07-2014	IFW SCAN & PACR AUTO SECURITY REVIEW
11-07-2014	ENTITY STATUS SET TO UNDISCOUNTED (INITIAL DEFAULT SETTING OR STATUS CHANGE)
11-07-2014	INITIAL EXAM TEAM

The veil of secrecy between inventor and the patent office keeps intellectual property intact while the claims make it through the gauntlet of submission, rejection, adjustment, and resubmission. I would have lost this patent, for example. Acquiescing to article 18.44.1 would have irreparably harmed U.S. inventors.

It's not as though the Obama administration even really denied that. On May 14, 2015, Congressman Brad Sherman (D-CA), in a hearing before the House Committee on Foreign Affairs, decried the United States as having "the largest trade deficit the world has ever seen 20 years in a row" despite having the best workforce.[3] He and Republican Congressman Dana Rohrabacher (R-CA), were grilling Charles Rivkin, then assistant secretary of state for economic and business affairs, and Assistant Secretary Daniel Russel of the State Department's Bureau of East Asian and Pacific Affairs on human rights issues concerning workers in Vietnam.

"Why do the best lose?" asked Congressman Sherman. "Because we—for 20 years, we have had the worst trade policy in the world, and now we are asked to double down on it. We are told that our trade deficit gets better with free trade agreements. That is simply false."[4]

Sherman cited figures showing that American trade deficits have grown more than 425 percent with nations that we have free trade agreements with. Prior promises that free trade agreements *wouldn't* increase America's trade deficit always seem to fall apart upon contact with reality, he complained.

Then, speaking of the Trans-Pacific Partnership, he said:

Every lobbyist in Washington whose job it is to create higher profits is telling us to vote for the deal, and every Representative in Washington whose job it is to create higher wage is telling us to vote no on the deal. Maybe they [wage warriors] are right.

We are given the straw man that the choices between the present system where we go into negotiations with the lowest tariffs in the world, or get going with a trade deal that is even worse. Real trade negotiation would be you start and you go in and you threaten to increase our tariffs. You put us on an equal playing field in the negotiations. You don't re-announce your surrender.[5]

Congressman Sherman almost sounds like Donald Trump there! And that's how it should be. Under our system, the legislature is supposed to hold the executive to account. When Congress fails to do its job, Americans suffer.

Comments from Congressman Rohrabacher were even better.

Mr. ROHRABACHER. Prior to this—let me ask both of our witnesses, I take it that both of you have—could you tell me just a yes or no, you have actually read this agreement, TPP, have you read the agreement?

Ambassador RIVKIN. Sir, my trade——

Mr. ROHRABACHER. May I have a yes or no?

Ambassador RIVKIN. I am fully briefed on the agreement, but I have not read——

Mr. ROHRABACHER. You have not read it. Have you read it? That is enough.

Have you read it?

Mr. RUSSEL. I have read the parts that are relevant.

Mr. ROHRABACHER. No you haven't. I am not saying the parts, have you read the agreement as it stands now? Neither one of them have done that. Let's be very clear, you have been here testifying about all these magnificent things and you haven't even read the agreement.[6]

Congressman Rohrabacher then exposed what the TPP would do to intellectual property.

Mr. ROHRABACHER. Okay, let me ask you again, from what you have read in this TPP, how does it affect intellectual property rights? Is there a provision now in TPP that you were advocating that tells us that we must publish our patent applications in the United States after 18 months whether or not the patent has been granted. Is that part of the TPP?

Ambassador RIVKIN. Sir, intellectual property rights are essential to any investment.

Mr. ROHRABACHER. I asked you a specific question on a specific part. Is there a provision in the TPP that mandates that intellectual property on the intellectual property rights area, that patent applications have to be published after 18 months, whether or not they have been granted—the patent has been granted?

Ambassador RIVKIN. The essence of investment has to do with transparency predictability and rule of law, and rule of law is clearly involved with intellectual property protections——

Mr. ROHRABACHER. Can you answer the question? I have given you a yes or no, you are here testifying about a treaty. I am asking you a specific on it, you have already told us you haven't even read it yet. Come on, is that part of the treaty?

Ambassador RIVKIN. We will get you a specific answer from USGR on your specific question.

Mr. ROHRABACHER. Well, I hope so, and I hope it is soon, because I have information, people have told me that something that we defeated here in this House 20 years ago, an attempt by huge multi- national corporations to change our patent law, they are still trying do it, but what we defeated 20 years ago they are trying to sneak into this treaty. And what it says, my fellow colleagues, is that after 18 months if we have an application for a patent, that patent has to be published whether or not it has been granted. I call that the Steal American Technologies Act, because it gives all of our competitors, all of these people that you had trust in with this TPP—the fact is all of them will have our utmost secrets, even before the patent has been granted and the person who has invented this has the right to defend that creation that belongs to him or her.[7]

Well. That's how it's done.

I can't thank Representative Rohrabacher enough for standing up for American inventors, workers, and citizens with that exchange. My heart was pounding out of my chest when I watched the YouTube video of the exchange. We elect our representatives to fight for us when we are at work earning the money that pays their salaries in the form of taxes. The citizens of California's Thirtieth and Forty-Eighth districts got their money's worth that day.

But the threat remains. Intellectual property is a bedrock of our prosperity. And it is under attack.

Pharmaceutical innovations are also threatened by the TPP treaty. Currently a U.S. patent holder will receive a twenty-year patent on a product, less the time between filing and issuance of said patent. Article 18.51.1 would reduce that term to eight years for pharmaceuticals and five years for biologics. Time is money.

How many hard-to-patent drugs do you think manufacturers are going to sink large sums of money into with such short payback periods? Way fewer is the answer.

Who will suffer for that? People who suffer from rare illnesses. That's not just an ethical dilemma but a real-life business decision. If a pharmaceutical company goes out of business, they help no one.

There are some elements of the treaty that acknowledge the importance of intellectual property. For example, article 18.76.1 calls for nations to confiscate counterfeit materials and prevent the release of products with confusing trademarks. This is obviously a good thing, but how is it to be enforced when we can't even prevent masses of people from crossing our borders without being detained?

Obviously, I am on the side of copyright holders and want to ensure the integrity of ownership will be maintained. But as it stands today, the United States does not have control of its borders, and it seems likely counterfeit materials could slip through. What would happen then, were something like TPP or another international trade plan in place?

Depending on how trade disputes are supposed to be resolved, it could be a nightmare for American companies. As is already happening to Canada with NAFTA, and as would have happened to the United States under TPP, unelected tribunals staffed by foreigners could rule against American companies who do business overseas, what is known as "lawfare" in the legal profession.

Consider this example. A Malaysian film company produces a film and releases it locally and it does so-so in the local Malay market. An enterprising person says, "I can get you $10 million if you will give me a master of the film." The film company agrees, so the go-getter brings the film to the United States and manages to distribute copies. Then, the Malay film company gets attorneys to file a lawsuit claiming that they expected to make $20 million in the U.S. market and American law enforcement didn't do enough to prevent pirating.

Sound crazy? Maybe so, but the mechanisms are now all in place to enable a swindle of whichever American jurisdiction they decide to go after. Maybe it will be Texas. Maybe it will be Wisconsin. There's no guarantee those who would decide are operating in good faith. That's the problem with creating monster trade deals that are guaranteed to spawn unintended consequences.

As it stands now, any case like this is decided in American courts and is guided by prior case law. It would be public, so we could see the actual procedure that is taking place. This system has worked for us for centuries. I see no reason to change it.

And I see no reason to change our intellectual property

system. The protection of intellectual property is explicitly guaranteed by our Constitution. As Dana Rohrabacher noted, there are those who have been trying to weaken these protections for decades now.

I see this as nothing but rebellion against the wishes of our Founding Fathers. We have to stand against any "Steal American Technologies Act," whether proposed openly or smuggled in under the guise of a trade agreement. Intellectual property is a key element of our continued prosperity. And political leaders in both parties need to defy the lobbyists and speak out in its defense.

9

OBAMACARE, RYANCARE, AND WHAT THE GOP SHOULD DO ON HEALTH CARE

FOR YEARS, THE REPUBLICAN PARTY has promised to repeal Obamacare. Fury at our prior president's disastrous health care bill helped inspire the Tea Party. It drove the Republican victories in midterm elections. It's led to the collapse of the Democratic Party nationwide.

Now, we have a Republican president, a Republican House, and a Republican Senate. No more excuses.

Repeal Obamacare and do not replace it. That's my position.

(Read on because in a few pages I'll make it even simpler with some help from a very dear friend, Ann Coulter.)

Do not convert any of the current programs into voucher programs. We should not be giving block grants from the federal government to states. That makes no sense. Let the states handle that through their own tax regimes and take the federal government out of it. Why should one state subsidize another, with Washington, DC, playing the role of dealer in a crooked game of three-card Monte?

Indeed, such programs only encourage fiscally irresponsible policies on the part of the states. If a state gets itself into fiscal trouble, especially with bloated retirement pensions they promise state workers and are unable to pay, they should deal with it themselves. We can't have every state get a federal bailout, like Puerto Rico did in the situation I described in chapter 3. Paul Ryan, of course, denied it was a bailout, but what else would you call subsidizing a failed local government with the taxes of other citizens?[1] If a state's citizens insist on electing socialist politicians, they can pay socialist state taxes, which will send businesses fleeing to friendlier climates.

At the same time, President Trump was right to say during the campaign that we weren't going to mess with Social Security or Medicare or Medicaid. Do not privatize any of these programs, and forget any ridiculous schemes cooked up by some Conservatism Inc. nonprofit to dramatically change them. We want the Main Street economy to fund the continuation of these programs. We do not want the Wall Street economy to have any more sway over the future of our retirement or social programs than they already do. I completely oppose attempts to use Social Security funds to prop up Wall Street. I want a focus on the Main Street economy, with an emphasis on job creation programs, tariffs to protect American industries, and infrastructure investments.

I wish President Trump had followed my advice. Instead, incredibly, the Trump administration was immediately sucked into a destructive fight over health care. Rather than a flat repeal of Obamacare, we get Paul Ryan's American Health Care Act.

This bill is a political disaster. Like Obamacare, it's a giant handout to the insurance companies. The health giant Anthem has already come out in favor of it.[2] Rather than draining the swamp, we're subsidizing it. It actually increases health care costs for core Trump voters in Pennsylvania, Michigan, and my state of Wisconsin.[3] Older, white voters would be disproportionately hurt by the plan, and the AARP has already come out in opposition. The plan also phases out tax credits for middle-class voters who are already struggling to make ends meet.[4] It doesn't even include a plan to let people buy health insurance across state lines, as President Trump promised during the campaign. Instead, we are told this will be in "part 2."[5] Politically, it seems almost designed to destroy the Trump coalition. Frankly, I wouldn't put it past Paul Ryan.

According to Congressional Budget Office projections, a full repeal of Obamacare would actually mean more people are insured than under Ryancare.[6] Indeed, as Robert Laszewki, president of the health care consulting group Health Policy and Strategy Associates, put it before the election, stripping the mandates under Obamcare and repealing it would actually incentivize more Americans to sign up because it would allow companies to offer more flexible and cheaper plans.

"There has to be some incentive for people to sign up and the incentive that we have right now is a penalty," Laszewski said. "Democrats make this big deal about (the Affordable Care Act) covering 20 million people but what they don't tell you is only 40 percent of the subsidy eligible are signed up. Trump will attract more people by making it more possible for insurance companies to offer health plans that are much more flexible by not having the rigid plan designs we have under the Affordable Care Act now.[7]

Instead, Ryancare gives us the worst of both worlds. As Philip Klein at the *Washington Examiner* has noted, "The Republican replacement preserves many of Obamacare's regulations that drive up the cost of insurance. So, in essence, the GOP alternative would be asking people to purchase expensive Obamacare plans, with less financial assistance."[8] This is political suicide and idiotic policy. And Speaker Ryan is targeting members of his own party who hesitated to vote for it.[9]

Of course, much of our money is already being spent on dealing with illegal immigrants who shouldn't even be in the country. Illegal immigration costs U.S. taxpayers about $113 billion a year at the federal, state, and local levels. The bulk of the costs—some $84 billion—are absorbed by state and local governments.[10]

That is a 2013 estimate and based on 13 million illegal aliens in this country. The number is certainly higher now, as are the costs. And Zack Taylor, chairman of the National Association of Former Border Patrol Officers, said in a letter that the number of illegal immigrants in the country is probably closer to 20 million.[11]

If that 20 million number is correct, the cost isn't $113 billion per year; it is closer to $174 billion per year. After the border surges in the later Obama years, the cost is probably about $200 billion per year!

Corporations are not required to collect payroll taxes on certain classes of aliens, who, in turn, also do not pay these payroll taxes. In a report prepared in 2012, when the number of aliens in the represented classes was on the order of a half million alien workers, the Social Security, Medicare, and Federal Unemployment Tax Act (FUTA) trust funds losses were calculated at over $1.5 trillion per year.[12]

TRUST FUND LOSSES CAUSED BY THE HIRING OF FOREIGN WORKERS[13]

FOREIGN WORKER PROGRAM AND VISA TRUST	ESTIMATED YEARLY LOSS SUFFERED BY TRUST FUNDS
STATE DEPARTMENT SUMMER WORK TRAVEL PROGRAM (J-1)	$128,000,000[1]
OTHER EXCHANGE PROGRAMS (J-1)	$266,000[2]
FOREIGN STUDENTS (F-1, M-1) WORKING OFF-CAMPUS (CPT)	$266,000,000[3]
FOREIGN GRADUATES (F-1, M-1) OF U.S. COLLEGES (OPT)	$737,000,000[4]
CULTURAL EXCHANGE ("DISNEY VISAS" OR Q-1)	$3,400,000[2]
FOREIGN FARMWORKERS (H-2A) AND MOST H-2BS ON GUAM	$127,000,000[5]
TOTAL ANNUAL TRUST FUND LOSSES	$1,527,400,000

And yet Ryancare doesn't even prevent illegal immigrants from receiving taxpayer-subsidized health care. Indeed, it's actually worse than Obamacare in some respects! There is no provision for officials to check an enrollee's immigration status. Obamacare at least mandated that Health and Human Services and the IRS check the Social Security numbers of those applying for health care. However, because the budget reconciliation process is what Speaker Ryan is using to push his health care bill through, the bill can't include language mandating that Social Security numbers be checked under the new program.

Katie McHugh has noted, "What Republicans are doing is almost inexplicable: Ramping up the most punishing aspects of Obamacare while removing even its fig-leaf requirements against granting illegal aliens health care."[14]

Indeed, I find it hard to believe this is anything other than deliberate sabotage of President Trump by Speaker Paul Ryan. For Ryan to suggest that his plan represents the Donald Trump or GOP health care solution is disingenuous, especially given the broad distancing of rank-and-file House members from the document. Furthermore, I don't recall President Trump positioning the repeal of Obamacare in such a way that that it would blow up the Republican Party. Quite the contrary. President Trump has bent over backwards to unite the party. Just because of his political incompetence, Ryan should be forced to resign as Speaker.

Regarding how the GOP should move forward when it comes to health care, nobody in America should be forced to buy insurance. If students or young people choose to risk a bit of indentured servitude by forgoing purchasing insurance, then they will find themselves having to pay medical bills for quite some time. That's their choice. But if we repeal Obamacare, insurance companies will be able to present more varied plans, which will allow students and young people to obtain the coverage they need at a cheaper price.

I favor a full repeal. But given the choice between Obamacare and Ryancare, I say it's better to let them fail than to try to prop up a dysfunctional system and hurt our own constituents in the process. Ann Coulter had a brilliant idea, and I quote:

> STEP 1: Congress doesn't repeal Obamacare! Instead, Congress passes a law, pursuant to its constitutional power to regulate interstate commerce, that says: "In America, it shall be legal to sell health insurance on the free market. This law supersedes all other laws, taxes, mandates, coverage requirements, regulations or prohibitions, state or federal." The end. Love, Ann.[15]

But in the long run, the solution to the health care problem is connected to other issues. There are things we need to do on other fronts in order to free up resources to tackle health care. We have to bring good jobs, which include benefits, back to our country by rethinking our trade policies. We have to stop wasting money paying for illegal immigration. And we have to start putting our own citizens first by not blowing untold trillions on pointless foreign interventions.

And that's what I need to talk about next.

10

AN AMERICA FIRST FOREIGN POLICY

THE UNITED STATES OF America needs a fundamental shift in its foreign policy. For far too long, we have stationed troops around the world, intervened endlessly in the affairs of other nations, and spent a vast amount of blood and treasure. Sixteen years after September 11, we are still in Afghanistan, and even as this was being written, there was yet another report of one of our Afghan "allies" firing on our own soldiers.[1] The Middle East is still aflame, with the Syrian civil war raging on, Iraq still unstable, and Iran drawing ever closer to a nuclear bomb. And of course, our own borders are undefended.

What America lacks most is a real sense of priorities when it comes to our foreign policy. Instead, it seems we lurch from crisis to crisis, never really getting anywhere. Under Barack Obama (and Secretary of State Clinton), we actually made things worse. The ill-considered decision to overthrow the government of Libya led to the ongoing refugee crisis in Europe. The aid to supposed "rebels" in Syria (many of whom are linked to Islamic extremists, such as al-Qaeda) hasn't led to a new democracy in the Middle East, but a seemingly endless regional conflict that threatens to suck in the great powers. And even the situation in North Korea threatens to explode at any moment.

What makes matters worse are the neoconservatives in the Republican Party who seem utterly determined to get the United States in another war, any war, seemingly for no reason whatsoever. The leading figures are of course John McCain and Lindsey Graham. It's hard to avoid noticing how these two senators, so eager to send Americans to die to defend the borders of Ukraine, seem utterly indifferent or even hostile to the idea of defending our own border. And when western Europe seems to be transforming into just another part of the Muslim world, we continue to import impossibly vetted Muslim "refugees."

We can't go on like this. The establishment in both the Republican and Democratic parties are leading us to disaster. We need a new set of organizing principles to guide our country's conduct in the world, a grand strategy. Here is mine.

First, we need to look to the American past to guide our future contact. Just as we need to rediscover the lost tradition of American economic nationalism, we need to renew the

American tradition of foreign policy restraint. "Wherever the standard of freedom and independence has been or shall be unfurled, there will her heart, her benedictions and her prayers be," said President John Quincy Adams of America. "But she goes not abroad, in search of monsters to destroy. She is the well-wisher to the freedom and independence of all. She is the champion and vindicator only of her own."[2]

America's national interest should be the lodestar of our foreign policy. We need to reduce our international commitments and not be recklessly provoking fights with other nations. Nor should we be overthrowing foreign governments simply because they are not "democratic" by Western standards. If the history of the Middle East in the last ten years has taught us anything, it is that overthrowing an established autocracy sometimes only opens the door for a far more virulent and hateful tyranny.

Second, we need to rethink some of our alliances. For example, one of our supposed "allies" is Saudi Arabia. Who can forget the image of Barack Obama bowing before the king of Saudi Arabia or George W. Bush holding hands with the Saudi prince? American troops defended the independence of the kingdom in the first Persian Gulf War and have sold huge amounts of arms to the country in the years since. Yet it is Saudi Arabia that provides money and support to many of the extreme Islamic movements penetrating the West, notably the Wahabbists, which serve as the fountainhead for so many terrorist groups.[3] What kind of an ally is this?

Or consider Turkey. It's increasingly clear Turkish president Recep Tayyip Erdoğan is building an Islamist dictatorship in the once-secular country. He's holding the entire West hostage using refugees as a weapon and is openly declaring his intention to conquer nations such as Germany through demographic warfare.[4] Evidence also suggests Turkey has been providing support to ISIS, using as a proxy to attack the Kurds.[5] Yet Turkey is a NATO ally. Is this really a nation our armed forces should be sworn to defend?

Third, we need to rethink some of our enemies. Since the election, the media and the Democrats have been obsessed with Russia and the idea that Vladimir Putin "hacked" the election. Of course, now Democrats are quietly realizing the massive conspiracy theory they had used to explain their shocking election defeat probably doesn't hold water.[6] Still, for some reason, the media, the Democrats, and several Republicans seem utterly determined to start a new Cold War with Russia.

The more likely scenario is that Putin is using the Muslim networks developed by Nazi Germany during World War II and refined by Soviets as a proxy against the United States. However, the mainstream media wouldn't touch that with a ten-foot pole.

Most of all, our leaders seem blind, deliberately so, to what is the great geopolitical development of our times, the Islamization of Europe. Entire neighborhoods in France and Sweden are essentially lost to law enforcement in what are called "no go zones."[7] Kurds and Turks fight on the streets of German cities. And everywhere, security services are stretched to the brink waiting for the next terrorist attack. Worrying about Russian influence in Montenegro seems positively obscene when our children may have to confront the reality of an Islamic France or a Muslim-run United Kingdom. Shouldn't we at least be considering how that will change our strategic situation?

As a grand strategy, I believe America should be the bulwark of the Judeo-Christian West. We should work to lessen tensions with Russia and promote stability in the Middle East and the Third World, rather than starting wars to spread "democracy." We should work with Asian allies to contain North Korea as best we can and maintain a strong Navy to rebut Chinese expansionism. Finally, we should stand up for our own national interests above all. Foreign aid and funding to groups such as the United Nations needs to be secondary to the welfare of our own people.

Yet there's something more fundamental than all of that. The protection of our own borders. Before we even have a discussion about Russia or ISIS, we need to talk about California, Arizona, and New Mexico.

As I saw firsthand during my trip to the border, drug cartels are operating within our own territory. Mexico is on the brink of being a failed state because of the way cartels can corrupt Mexican law enforcement, slaughter journalists, and essentially operate as a government unto themselves. We cannot allow such groups to gain any more power within our own territory. We cannot allow the horrid scenes of beheadings and torture that are now typical in Mexico to come here. A border wall is just as fundamental—perhaps even more fundamental—to our national security as a strong army or a great naval fleet. Also, as discussed before, we need extreme vetting to ensure we are not importing future terrorist threats through a misguided "refugee" program.

Contra what was proposed in TPP, I do not think we should be discussing our border security policies with any other nation. As President Trump has so often said, we need a "great wall," but we need more than that. We need to give our brave Border Patrol officers the support they need. We need to make sure we have defenses against tunneling and attempts at infiltration by sea. Most important, we need to make sure we have however many skilled personnel are required to guard our territory. If we can't even defend our own borders, what is the point of even having armed services? Indeed, if our government won't defend our borders, arguably its primary responsibility, why do we have to pay so much in taxes?

Other threats to our national security can't be fought with bombs or bullets. One of the most dire is the threat of a pandemic enabled by our lax border controls. National security is compromised when we bring foreigners to America that carry diseases that are atypical for the United States. Tuberculosis, measles, whooping cough, mumps, scarlet fever, and bubonic plague were all but eradicated from American life, but they are now on the rise across certain areas of our country.[8] Uncontrolled migration from nations with sizable unvaccinated populations is practically inviting disaster.

As this was being written, the courts had once again rejected President Trump's attempt for a temporary travel ban on those from certain Islamic countries. The reasoning behind this decision is positively dangerous. U.S. District Judge Derrick Watson in Hawaii, a former classmate of Barack Obama who had met with the former president only hours before, claimed the ban "was issued with a purpose to disfavor a particular religion." The ban didn't actually refer to any religion and was a temporary restriction on all immigration from certain terror-linked countries. However, both Watson and U.S. District Judge Theodore D. Chuang in Maryland reached outside the evidence of the dispute itself and used campaign statements from President Trump and his advisers to say the executive order was an attempt at the "Muslim ban" promised during the campaign and therefore could not be allowed.

As author Daniel Horowitz has noted, Watson is essentially declaring that the president and even Congress are simply not allowed to impose any restrictions on immigration because of a newly discovered "global freedom of religion," and that any restriction on immigration that disproportionately affects Muslims is somehow unconstitutional. (Needless to say, I doubt the courts would protest any restriction that disproportionately harms Christians.) What the courts are really doing is inventing, out of whole cloth, a right for the entire Muslim world to immigrate to the United States. They are also completely gutting the lawful authority of the president.[9] It's worth noting that the seven nations President Trump targeted in his initial plan have produced seventy-two people convicted of terrorism.[10]

Our position should be clear. Only American citizens have the absolute right to be in the United States. As President Trump said to Angela Merkel, the woman who has all but destroyed her nation in the name of open borders, immigration is a privilege, not a right. And even American citizens can have their citizenship revoked for falsification or concealment of relevant facts while applying for citizenship, refusal to testify before Congress, a dishonorable military discharge, and membership in subversive groups.[11]

On that last note, we need to discuss the Muslim Brotherhood. It is my position that the Muslim Brotherhood should be designated a terrorist group by President Trump. During an investigation of the group by the FBI, law enforcement found a document titled "Explanatory Memorandum on the General Strategic Goal for the Group in North America," which detailed the plans for a "grand jihad in eliminating and destroying the Western civilization from within and 'sabotaging' its miserable house by their hands and by the hands of the believers so that it is eliminated and God's religion is made victorious over all other religions."[12] I can't conceive of a more obvious smoking gun. And it's worth noting that the plaintiff in one of the cases that led to President Trump's travel ban being tossed out by the courts was an imam with ties to the Muslim Brotherhood.[13]

National security has to begin with border security. Crimes by illegal immigrants are a national security threat. There should be no crimes by illegal immigrants in our country, because there should be no illegal immigrants in our country. Similarly, we should not be actually importing potential terrorist threats. They used to say, "We have to fight them there so we don't have to fight them here." But I can't help but notice that those who seem the most eager to pick fights overseas also seem to be the most willing to invite threats here.

Because of my interest in trade, I also consider the safety of our food supply to be an important part of national security. It's something I have direct experience in because of my career. Here in the United States, dairy products stamped "Grade A" are subject to inspections by the Department of Agriculture, either by the federal inspectors or the state inspectors, or both. For many years I manufactured equipment that bore the Pasteurized Milk Ordinance seal. That equipment was subject to harsh testing and cleanability analysis for clean-in-place operation to ensure no pathogenetic food contamination would ensue with proper operation of the facility, and even extending to chain-of-custody handling of food product. Food-processing facilities across the nation are inspected daily and logs of operation are maintained so that any food-borne illness is tracked back to the source rapidly to prevent sickness and loss of life.

One of the things that infuriated me most about TPP was how it would have undermined our food safety regulations. It didn't provide a way to ensure food from other nations would met our standards. It would be all but impossible to impose the kind of tracking regime required to contain an outbreak resulting from ill-prepared food shipped by another country. Ensuring our food supply is safe seems to me to be as much a national security issue as a trade issue.

Yet another national security issue is our energy policy. As the need to secure our energy supply is also at the root of many of our foreign policy decisions, energy policy should also be viewed from a national security standpoint. Here, there are some signs we are moving in the right direction. Despite the Obama administration's emphasis on "green energy," our economy runs on petroleum and gas. Fracking has tilted the playing field in a decidedly American direction.

We now have leverage that for decades evaded us. We should stop funding regimes that seek to destroy our country. I would work to reduce the amount of money we send to regimes such as Saudi Arabia. I fervently hope the Trump administration does the same. Personally, I would like to see America move toward an embrace of nuclear power. France derives roughly 75 percent of their electricity from nuclear power. The French run on the latest technology, and a whopping 17 percent of their electricity is produced from recycled nuclear fuel.[14] While the management of nuclear waste is a challenge, it is not unmanageable. But making this possible will require President Trump to roll back a regulatory regime that has stifled new reactor approvals for more than a decade.

An America First foreign policy means starting with protecting and developing our homeland and working outward. We need to guard our borders and the physical safety of our people. We need to form productive relationships with foreign nations with which we have common ground. We need to repudiate commitments to nations such as Saudi Arabia and Turkey that wish us ill. And as with trade, we need to use America's leverage as the world's foremost economic power and, increasingly, as the world's energy superpower, to reduce our dependence on and vulnerability to foreign powers.

I believe in America first, last, and only. And frankly, if others don't feel the same way, I don't know what they are even doing here.

THE NEW RIGHT, THE NEW MEDIA, AND A TRUMP GOP

IT WAS LATE AFTERNOON and I had just left an education forum in Kenosha. Looking at my phone, I saw what looked to be like a tweet from . . . What the—

Donald J. Trump ✓
@realDonaldTrump

  👤⁺ Follow

Thanks to @pnehlen for your kind words, very much appreciated.

RETWEETS   LIKES
4,633   15,164

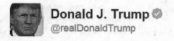

© twitter

My phone started to blow up with the retweets. Without a whole lot of thought about it, I gave a simple honest reply.

The controversy that ensued from that tweet exchange would fuel outrage in the GOP leadership, not to mention frantic speculation in the news media. The barrage of questions came fast and furious. I was disappointed about how few of these questions were about the issues involved in the campaign: immigration, TPP, and national security. Instead, there was only the focus on the battle of personalities between then candidate Donald Trump and Paul Ryan.

Of course, there were some rare reporters who actually did ask about substantive issues, both at this time and throughout the campaign. Talk show host Lars Larson asked me about trade, open borders, and the omnibus spending bill. Steve Bannon and Alex Marlow at Breitbart asked me about trade, open borders, refugee resettlement, and so many other issues. Tammy Bruce would grill me on a variety of different things, as did Laura Ingraham. Alex Jones is often mocked by the mainstream media as "fake news," but it was Jones who asked probing questions about national sovereignty and immigration and who actually dedicated the time needed to discuss these subjects substantively on InfoWars.com. Charles C. Johnson over at GotNews.com asked probative questions. Andrew Wilkow was outstanding on *The Wilkow Majority*, as was Wayne Dupree on *The Wayne Dupree Show*. And Lou Dobbs was the one interviewer on a major network who wanted to have a discussion about trade and immigration. Locally, John "Sly" Sylvester and the guys at *The Devil's Advocate*, Mike Crute and Dominic Salvia, represented engaged citizenship in the best American tradition.

But for the rest of the mainstream media, it was Donald

Trump's tweet and my response that was most compelling. And the whole thing started because of something I believe was a phony issue.

As you undoubtedly remember during the 2016 Democratic National Convention, Khizr Khan, an immigration lawyer[1] and the father of fallen soldier Captain Humayun Khan, took to the stage to condemn Donald Trump. The media covered it as a political masterstroke. When Donald Trump defended himself, the result was outrage from liberal journalists, as if it were somehow illegitimate for Trump to rebut a political attack made literally from the stage of an opposing party's political convention. Paul Ryan and Mitch McConnell both issued mealy-mouthed statements that did not defend their party's nominee and wouldn't even name Donald Trump.[2]

This cowardly response disgusted me. So this is what I put up on my website:

Khizr Khan Ignores Recent History and Reality in Convention Attack on Donald Trump

(Paul Nehlen)—Liberals and the mainstream media are having a collective meltdown, verging on an aneurism, over Donald Trump responding to the political attack launched against him at the Democrats' convention last week by the father of a Muslim-American soldier who was killed in Iraq.

Without doubt, Khizr and Ghazala Khan's son—Captain Humayun Khan—is an American hero who gave his life in defense of the United States of America while serving in Iraq in 2004. Our nation owes Capt. Khan and his Gold Star parents a debt that can never be repaid.

However . . .

Mr. and Mrs. Khan chose to politicize the death of their son when they appeared on-stage in support of Hillary Clinton at the Democrat National Convention in Philadelphia. Indeed, in his remarks Mr. Khan attacked, ridiculed and attempted to humiliate Mr. Trump and his positions on critical national security issues.

Did he really think his attack would go unanswered?

It's not my place to respond on behalf of Mr. Trump; however, there are facts related to this controversy that the media clearly—and intentionally, in my opinion—isn't telling the public about. So allow me . . .

Mr. Khan charged that under Donald Trump's proposed TEMPORARY suspension of refugee resettlements from specific Muslim countries, Capt. Khan "never would have been in America." But this is comparing apples to oranges.

In fact, the Khans moved to the United States from Pakistan in the 1970s. That was long before the 9/11 radical Muslim attacks on the Twin Towers and Pentagon changed everything in this country.

And Capt. Khan's death came years before the Ft. Hood shooting, the Boston Marathon bombing, the Chattanooga killings, the San Bernardino Christmas party mass murder and the Orlando nightclub massacre.

Circumstances have clearly and dramatically changed in the U.S. since Capt. Khan's death at the hands of a Muslim suicide bomber in Iraq.

In addition, just because Capt. Khan was a patriotic Muslim-American who loved and fought for his adopted country, that doesn't mean other Muslim-Americans don't hate the United States and wish our people deadly harm.

A research paper, "Muslim-American Involvement with Violent Extremism, 2015" by Charles Kurzman of the Department of Sociology at the University of North Carolina, Chapel Hill details some facts Mr. Khan and his supporters in the media are overlooking . . .

1. Muslim-Americans have been fighting on BOTH sides of the war. In fact, more Muslim-Americans (20) have been killed since 9/11 fighting for ISIS than have been killed fighting for America (14).
2. Since 9/11, the number of Muslim-Americans who have been killed in action fighting for the U.S. is the same as the number of American soldiers who have been killed by fellow Muslim-American soldiers Major Nidal Hasan at Ft. Hood and Sgt. Hasan Akbar at Camp Pennsylvania in Kuwait.
3. Since 9/11, the number of Muslim-Americans who have been killed fighting for terrorist organizations in Syria, Iraq, Somalia, Yemen, and Pakistan is almost three times the number of Muslim-Americans who have been killed in action fighting for the U.S.

In addition . . .

- According to a February 2015 report in The Hill, "FBI Director James Comey revealed that his agency is investigating suspected supporters of the Islamic State in Iraq and Syria (ISIS) in every state across the U.S."
- According to a July 2015 report in The Hill, "the FBI told Senate lawmakers that more than 200 Americans have tried to join Islamic extremists in Iraq and Syria."

- According to a November 2015 report by Judicial Watch, "The Federal Bureau of Investigation (FBI) has nearly 1,000 active probes involving the terrorist group Islamic State of Iraq and Syria (ISIS) inside the United States."

While the media focuses on a nebulous "small number" of Muslim "lone wolf terrorists," the real breakpoint is the much larger subset of Muslims compliant to Islam's laws of shariah.

Polls have put the numbers of "American Muslims" who believe they should have a choice between U.S. Law and shariah over the 50% mark. That is a big number of potential terrorists.

Mr. and Mrs. Khan shouldn't have tragically lost their son to a Muslim suicide bomber while protecting his fellow American soldiers in Iraq.

But the murderous radical Islamic enemy that his candidate, Hillary Clinton, refuses to name is increasingly operating on our shores.

And no American citizens should lose their lives—or the lives of their sons and daughters—to radical Muslim extremists while running a marathon, attending a Christmas party or dancing at a nightclub.

These are, indeed, desperate times.

But Mr. Trump's proposals aren't desperate measures. They're just common sense.[3]

This was what Donald Trump responded to and this is what created the media frenzy. But I was amazed how utterly uninterested the journalists were in the substance of what I had written. There were no questions about terrorism, about immigration, or about a long-term strategy to defeat radical Islam. Instead, the vast majority of reporters simply wanted to emphasize the fights within the Republican Party.

On a broader level, the media never addressed any of the points I made in my defense of Donald Trump, nor did they explain why Trump needed to meekly accept being slammed by Khan. Instead, we heard an endless repetition of slogans, about how Trump had supposedly attacked a Gold Star family when he had simply hit back in a fight that someone else started.[4] Khan later said that he was tired of the media attention and wanted to return to private life—but I saw the media trotting him out seemingly every week until Election Night and even beyond. He only recently fell from grace when he absurdly claimed he couldn't address an event in Canada because "his travel privileges are being reviewed," with the implication that the Trump administration had something to do with it. Needless to say, there was no evidence for this claim.[5]

Donald Trump popularized the term "fake news." It's not just that the media sometimes reports things that never happened. While that occurs, it's relatively easy to call out. What is really fake news are these narratives that the media promotes to suit their political agenda. The seemingly weeks-long firestorm over Khizr Khan was a typical example. Reporters simply declared Donald Trump's response immoral and unacceptable and then put an incredible amount of pressure on the Republican Party to disown him. None of this is really news—it's simply liberal activism.

Many journalists are simply activists in another guise. Their supposed reporting is really just a tactic to promote their political ends. Why, after all, should we regard the "reporting" of someone like CNN's Jake Tapper as anything different from a speech by someone like Nancy Pelosi?

And we are all familiar with the double standards. When illegal immigrants are deported, there are sob stories about breaking up families. But when an American is hurt or even killed by an illegal immigrant, anyone who notices it is accused of exploiting a tragedy. A crime is either a national story or buried in local news depending on the racial or sexual identity of the perpetrator and the victim. Links, no matter how marginal, to groups the liberal media considers "extreme" is career ending for conservatives. However, as the career of Keith Ellison shows, leftists can openly work with groups like the Nation of Islam or the Communist Party with no consequences.

This is why the general public distrusts the media. We know there is an agenda. We know they are pushing a narrative. And we know left wing journalists will attempt to hound and destroy anyone who opposes their agenda. Rather than seeking the truth, too many reporters operate like Communist commissars, seeking to hunt down and destroy anyone with dissident opinions.

This ordeal that's playing out with Susan Rice now with the unmasking is unbelievable. We're watching it unfold before our eyes, enmeshed with the fake news media personalities. Every unmasking, every single subsequent act in the chain of custody, or lack thereof, was a tyrannous act of terrorism. For President Trump and his American associates, family, you name it, surveilled by our own government for political reasons is beyond the pale. They were terrorized by our own government. Trump et al. were terrorized not unlike the conservative groups who were targeted by the IRS. This cannot go unpunished. Justice must be swift and severe, and include the news media if it can be proven they were complicit.

One of the main reasons Donald Trump won this presidential election is because so many Americans saw him as a way to strike back against the media. They were tired of being told on CNN and MSNBC what they were and were not allowed to think. They were bored with the hysterical lecturing and showy virtue signaling from pseudo-comedians such as Stephen Colbert, John Oliver, or Samantha Bee. They were disgusted at being lectured by degenerate celebrities on what is and is not moral. And they were nothing less than furious while witnessing reporters shamelessly, openly twist the facts and manipulate the audience's emotions in order to push a radical message.

Donald Trump, unlike just about any other Republican politician in history, didn't play by their rules. Whether in person or on Twitter, he always hit back. He never accepted the media's frame. He challenged the supposed neutrality of the press. He encouraged his supporters to see journalists for what they were: political activists working for his defeat. He knew that journalists' only interest was looking for a way to bring him down. Sadly, that is still the goal of many journalists—to take down our president with some invented scandal or outrageous attack.

Trump's "take no prisoners" tactics when it came dealing with the media seems to have emboldened an entire movement. Some have called it the alt-Right or the New Right. Young conservatives, nationalists, and right-wingers of all stripes merrily troll and scoff at the journalists who try to tell them what to think. They know these reporters are pushing an agenda, and they aren't going to fall for it. They won't be intimidated.

And neither will I. One of the first lessons I learned as a candidate is that the media is not your friend. Sometimes a journalist will pretend to be friendly and claim he is trying to hear "your side of the story," but it is usually just to get your guard down. What reporters are really looking for is the one unguarded comment or casual remark that they can twist to make you look bad. Again, most of them are just liberal activists, and their "journalism" is more a tactic than a profession.

Of course, there are some exceptions. There are a few I met during the campaign whom I am honored to have gotten to know. I consider them kindred spirits. I don't want to name them, because being a conservative in journalism can be as harmful to your career as being a conservative in Hollywood. But they know who they are.

What I consider to be real news is the struggle ordinary Americans are enduring to survive under a government that will not protect American jobs, stop illegal immigration, or provide succor to American communities. To me, an example of real news is the letter the Angel Moms group tried to present to Speaker of the House Paul Ryan, first in Washington, DC, and then at his home in Janesville, Wisconsin.

It read:

A Message To Paul Ryan From The American Victims Of Your Immigration Policies

Whereas Paul Ryan has a two-decade history of pushing for open borders

Whereas Paul Ryan defeated efforts in the 1990's to crack down on out-of-control immigration

Whereas Paul Ryan has fought valiantly on issues sought

by corporate special interests (such as the TPP), but has refused to make any similar public appeal on behalf of the American victims of illegal alien crime

Whereas Paul Ryan has enabled—whether through silence, indifference, complicity, or deceit—the implementation of President Obama's immigration agenda

Whereas Paul Ryan is personally responsible for the deaths, maimings, and sexual assaults of thousands of innocent Americans and lawful residents

Whereas Paul Ryan has never shown one millionth the passion in defense of our families as he has spent advocating for policies that would result in the deaths of more Americans

Whereas Paul Ryan has the blood of so many on his hands—blacks, whites, Asians, Hispanics, immigrants, and children of immigrants

Whereas Paul Ryan has used his positions of power—as a Republican Party leader, as a budget leader, as Speaker of the House, and as an intimate of large corporations with unlimited resources—to ignore and even undermine American interests. If Ryan's considerable powers had been marshaled, in any serious degree, towards advocating for our families, demanding change for our families, or insisting upon justice for our families, then so many more families just like us would have been saved.

For all of these reasons and more, we deem Ryan disqualified from serving in Congress or any other position of public office that is supposed to represent the American people

Today we issue Paul Ryan this ultimatum: Show contrition and make a commitment within the week to deliver on the following three items, or leave this race, resign this seat, and exit public life forever so you can do no more harm, cause no more damage, and inflict no more pain on one more family like ours.

We guarantee that any pain that Paul Ryan will experience from the loss of his cozy seat in Congress will pale by a factor of a million to the pain each and every one of us feel each and every day as a result of the loss we have endured—a loss from which we could have been spared had Paul Ryan only cared as much about us as he cares about his donors.

We are calling on Paul Ryan to

I. Return all of the donations he has received from individuals or groups that have lobbied for any kind of open borders immigration or amnesty policy.

II. Hold a press conference on the steps of the U.S. Capitol with Paul Ryan, the entire House Leadership team and the American victims of illegal alien crime. The press conference will call for the passage—in both chambers—of legislation to shut down every single sanctuary city in America, to make five year mandatory minimums for any one who re-enters the country illegally after previously being deported, and to make it an automatic felony for any one here illegally who is convicted of a separate, additional crime.

III. Guarantee that next year's budget will fully fund the completion of the 700 mile double layer border wall that Ryan's budget last year failed to fund, and pledge that in next year's budget, there will be no funding for any resettlement of illegal alien border crossers inside the interior of the United States.[6]

We all know Paul Ryan has done none of that. Chris Crane, president of the National Immigration and Customs Enforcement Council, said ICE officers "wish the speaker of the House would be more vocal in championing an immigration policy that defends the rule of law."[7]

Compare that to our new president, Donald Trump, a fighter who has declared he will turn the GOP into a "worker's party."[8] And Trump works hard. He acts as if he's in a competition every day. I recently watched a FiveThirtyEight animation of the campaign stops he and Hillary Clinton made on the campaign trail after each had won nomination.[9] It was brilliant. You could see candidate Trump hustling as he was jetting back and forth across the country. The dot representing Clinton looked sluggish in this time-lapsed sequence.

My expectations for the Trump administration is high. The fact that I supported candidate Trump in his quest to win the presidency doesn't mean I'm going to expect less because he was the guy I was pulling for. That would be foolish. As long as I'm able, I'll continue to monitor and advise from outside of Washington, DC. That's the essence of citizenship in this American republic. If I think something is going the wrong direction, I'll speak up. If there's a group that seems to be moving in the wrong direction, I'll voice my opposition, be they Democrats or Republicans.

But I trust Donald Trump because of my personal experience with the man. I know Mr. Trump didn't turn away from the pain of these families, those Angel Moms (and Dads). He worked for them. He fought for them. He put them on the campaign stage to help him crusade for the rights and safety of American citizens. And that's just what any responsible American official should do.

Taking care of our citizens is our oath.

Along with families from the Remembrance Project, I went to an event attended by Donald Trump on September 17, 2016. Then candidate Trump spoke to about four hundred guests. Before his speech, Trump met with the families along with my wife, me, and several other organizers and activists who had been working with the Remembrance Project.

Mr. Trump sat in that room for forty-five minutes asking questions of the families and intently listening to their replies. At one point, a young girl maybe ten years old approached Mr. Trump to give him a small token of her appreciation. Mr. Trump stood as she addressed him. When she tried to speak, all she could get out was a small squeak. Then she began to quietly sob.

As a compassionate father would do, Donald Trump pulled her close and gave her a hug to comfort her. There wasn't a dry eye in that room.

When it was time to go out to the main auditorium, Mr. Trump was asked by one of the family members to have a photo taken. With the effortless grace I've come to see as typical of the man, he took the time to allow all of the families to line up and have their photo taken with our future president.

My wife and I waited until all the families had the opportunity to get their photo with Mr. Trump and then made our way over. Political adviser Stephen Miller stepped over to me and said it might be a bad idea if I were to be photographed with Mr. Trump so close to the election. After all, Donald Trump needed to unite the Republican Party, and the last thing he needed was to spark further excitable media reporters about infighting between the Republican Party's leader in Congress and its presidential candidate. I told Stephen I understood completely. I just wanted to thank Mr. Trump for all he's done for the country, and Stephen said that was fine.

As we approached, I extended my hand and, with my back squarely to the camera, I said, "Mr. Trump, my name is Paul Nehlen, and I want to thank you for everything you've done, and are doing, for our country."

Trump responded, "I know who you are. You ran a great race up there in Wisconsin."

When I turned and introduced my wife, he reiterated, "He ran a great race, didn't he?"

We spoke briefly for a few minutes. I had him sign a copy of Ann Coulter's book *In Trump We Trust* before we parted.

As we crossed the conference room and were headed to the exit, we heard someone holler, "Paul!" My wife and I both spun on our heels. And there was Donald Trump with his thumb in the air. "Paul—great job," he said. "I mean it."

As we waved and turned into the main hallway leading to the main ballroom, I looked at my wife with an expression of shock. "He didn't have to do that," I said. "He didn't have to holler to us as we were walking out of that room."

She smiled and simply said, "No, you're right. He didn't have to do that. But he wanted to."

Those are the simple acts of kindness that don't get reported in the news. And it's those acts that transform a politician into a leader, a leader who knows how to wage the battle. Donald Trump, our president, is just such a man.

AN AMERICAN BIRTHRIGHT

*And for the support of this Declaration, with a firm reliance on the pro-
tection of divine Providence, we mutually pledge to each other our Lives,
our Fortunes, and our sacred Honor.*

—THE UNANIMOUS DECLARATION OF THE THIRTEEN UNITED
STATES OF AMERICA

AND WITH THAT LINE your birthright was cast in history. The
nation hadn't yet been won. But at that moment, the men who
bravely signed the Declaration of Independence were letting the
world know they were all in.

Are you all in?

The battle lines of globalism versus nationalism are drawn.

As you can see from this book, my battle to defeat the worst
trade deal in the history of the United States may have seemed

an impossible task—but we won.

We won not because I lied about the deal, or because I had unlimited resources with which to wage the battle against the globalist cabal inside the halls of Congress.

We won because we spoke truth to power.

We won because we shined the light of truth into the dark recesses of American politics.

We won because as it was for the signers of the Declaration, it was my duty, as an American citizen, to stand for nationalism over globalism, to stand for my fellow Americans who work every day to provide for their families, and who count on their elected representatives to obey their sacred oath of office. It was to defy that siren call of globalism.

It is for them that I waged the battle. And I'm not done fighting. I hope you'll join me.

ACKNOWLEDGMENTS

FIRST, THANK YOU TO MY WIFE, who had to spend an inordinate amount of time on the other side of a door while I plowed through research and wrote and rewrote sections, in hopes it would be a provoking story, compelling others to wage the battle.

I'd like to thank next Michael Thompson at WND, who reached out to me when I was about 95 percent complete with the first rendition of this book. He contacted me and was so enthusiastic with the project and introduced me to a wonderful group of people over at the WND organization. One of the first I would meet is Geoffrey Stone, who proceeded to eviscerate the book in the nicest way possible. I'm deeply indebted to Geoffrey for his thoughtful and patient understanding for the engineer trying to message to the masses. Thank you both. The receiving end of this eviscerated transcript was me and Kevin DeAnna. Reassembling and putting engineer-speak into what I hope you found to be compelling narrative was heavy lifting. I'm very grateful for his efforts.

Thank you to my friend and confidant Ron Maxwell, who doesn't have the time to be a mentor, yet finds the time nonetheless to read my writing and make suggestions.

Special thanks to Ben Cassady, who also doesn't have the time, but makes time.

There were so many kind people who endorsed my campaign. It's not something you intuitively think about when you're considering a run for office. At least it wasn't for me. To be sure, it is important that others give you their blessing with an endorsement, and that's what it is: their blessing. If you get an endorsement because it was forced, it wasn't their blessing. So many veterans endorsed me I can't even name them all here. God bless all of you.

One veteran I must make a point to acknowledge is a local here in Delavan, Wisconsin. His name is Joseph Guido, and he has a fascinating life story. We met as Joe was headed into the local library, and I'll never forget after introducing myself, Joe said, "Young man, you can't win an election by following old guys like me into the library." He then produced a few newspaper clippings to show me he was following the race, on my side. Thank you, and God bless you and Mary.

When I spoke to John Molloy, chairman of the National Vietnam and Gulf War Veterans Coalition, it was one of the proudest moments of my campaign. John already knew that I'd been an advisory board member for Operation Homefront and had advocated for our troops. His concerns were met, and that was a very humbling phone call, to be sure. I've carried his letter with me every day since I received it late in May 2016. It's probably time I put it in a frame on the wall.

One of the first public figures to endorse me was former governor Sarah Palin. She is a force to be reckoned with and has given such momentum, not just to my campaign, but to many others as well. She ratcheted my name recognition up significantly very early on.

Michelle Malkin was also an early supporter. Michelle, John Miano, and Sara Blackwell came to the area in April just after Abbott Labs laid off more than 150 IT workers who were replaced with less-skilled foreign workers through the H-1B visa program. Some of these workers live in Wisconsin's First Congressional District. Many other Abbott Labs workers who live in the district were also terror stricken at the thought of losing their jobs to H-1B workers. These three warriors work on behalf of American workers. Michelle led off my first public event in Kenosha and did a magnificent job.

Special thanks to Brandon Darby over at Breitbart Texas, who risked taking me and two other reporters out along the Texas border. Brandon's passion for supporting our law enforcement officers at all levels and branches of service, local and national, was something to behold.

Thanks to Stephen K. Bannon for assembling a team of honey badgers over at Breitbart and holding them to the high standards he holds for himself. Their coverage of my race delved into the issues, something the rest of the media failed to do.

Very special thanks to Sheriff Oscar Carrillo and Sheriff Arvin West and their deputies and their families for making the sacrifice to defend American soil every single day. Culberson and Hudspeth counties are better—America is better—for your efforts.

I had the distinct pleasure of meeting with Richard Viguerie over lunch in his office. Imagine sitting across the table from such an American conservative icon. He was terribly engaging and very kind with his suggestions and his planning advice. On his side table was a photo of him with fellow conservatives Phyllis Schlafly and Lee Edwards. Now, that's a power photo!

While I did not have the pleasure of meeting Phyllis Schlafly, I was fortunate to bring her a Nehlen for Congress shirt and get it to one of her staff at the Weyrich Lunch. As reported by Breitbart News: Schlafly explained that Ryan has repeatedly demonstrated that he is "not really for America" and is "not for American citizens." "Get rid of him! We don't want anybody who believes in open borders," Schlafly told Breitbart. "Obviously, Paul Ryan is not an 'America first' guy." Schlafly further explained that if Speaker Ryan cannot get in line with the majority of the American electorate on immigration, he "should resign." We should not "accept him as Speaker," Schlafly added—noting that, given Ryan's constant efforts to undermine his party's nominee, "it doesn't sound like he is loyal to the Republican Party."

Ms. Schlafly passed away on September 5, 2016. She knew that I hadn't beaten Paul Ryan in that primary, but also knew that we had derailed TPP. I'm sure she was smiling down on

Mr. Trump and his family as they walked out onto the stage in the wee hours of November 9 as our new president-elect!

Ann Coulter was one to say that she doesn't give endorsements because they sound "self-important." I love Ann Coulter. She couldn't give a damn about what her haters say. She speaks the truth and doesn't sugarcoat it. She's brilliant, brave, and beautiful. She graciously campaigned on my behalf on radio and here with me in the district on more than one occasion. Her words were true and directly on point. What more could you ask for? Not. One. Thing.

Lastly, I'd like to thank President Trump and his family for sticking it out and waging the battle for America First.

ANGEL MOMS SPEECH OUTSIDE RYAN'S WALLED MANSION

I'm Paul Nehlen and I'm running for Congress in the First Congressional District of Wisconsin to take back our district from the global special interests who control Paul Ryan.

Paul Ryan is the most open borders, pro–Wall Street, anti-worker member of Congress in either party.

Everything that Americans despise about their government, Paul Ryan represents.

Ryan is the embodiment of special-interest control, lies,

deception, corruption, contempt for the people, and the desire to curry favor and approval from faraway media elites while disregarding the feelings and aspirations of one's own constituents.

Paul Ryan represents arrogance, condescension, and the cultivation of a phony Washington image in place of true sincerity, conviction, and connection with common men and women.

I am not only running against Paul Ryan, but I'm running against an entire system of corporate control over our government that has disenfranchised every single voter in Wisconsin, and millions more across the nation.

Paul Ryan has sold out his district to his corporate masters. On August 9, the voters of Wisconsin have an historic opportunity: vote Ryan out and declare your freedom.

To the voters of Wisconsin, I say: August 9 is Wisconsin's Independence Day.

But before going further, I want to address the carnage and bloodshed that has taken place in Dallas, Texas.

Law and order is breaking down in America. Too many innocent people are living in fear and terror, while the elites, who have created this state of chaos, live comfortably behind their walls, fences, and gates.

That's why today—as our police officers across the nation are under attack, and our citizens suffer the consequences of crime spiraling out of control—I'm calling on Paul Ryan to bring up for an emergency vote making the attempted execution of a police officer a federal hate crime punishable by death in all fifty states, thus ensuring that any time a police officer is killed, the murderer will face the maximum penalty under the law, and the full resources of the federal government will be brought to bear to bring that person and his accomplices to justice.

I call on Ryan to hold this vote within the next seven days.

The stakes of Wisconsin's August 9 election cannot be overstated. One month from today, the voters of Wisconsin have the chance to take back their government and reclaim the people's house.

Never have any people of any district had such an extraordinary opportunity to reset the balance of power in America.

But Paul Ryan and his deep-pocket donors want you to believe this isn't so. They want you to believe that your vote doesn't matter. They want you to believe that Paul Ryan is Speaker of the House, and there is nothing you can do about it.

Yet, as Mr. Brat's victory in Virginia two years ago demonstrates, no big moneyed corporate donor, no transnational elite, no Washington politician can tell the American people what they must tolerate and who will rule over them.

Don't let anyone tell you that you can't have the kind of representation you want. Don't let anyone tell you that you aren't entitled to a Speaker who stands up for your voice and your family. Don't let anyone tell you that you're stuck with a leader who doesn't think your family deserves to be protected from terrorism, or open borders, or transnational gangs, or violent criminals.

With your vote on August 9, you can save your country from rule by corporate elites.

With your vote on August 9, you can dethrone the entire ruling class of America.

New reports say that in 2017 Congress plans to revive the disastrous Gang of Eight immigration agenda. With your vote on August 9, you have a chance to save your entire country from open borders.

New reports say that after November, Congress will move to ratify the job-destroying Trans-Pacific Partnership. With your vote on August 9, you can save your entire country from globalism. You can save your entire country from ceding sovereignty to the TPP's global governing commission.

On August 9, you have the power to kick out of Washington every corporate executive who thinks American workers are rubes and simpletons who are unworthy of their time and interest.

On August 9, you can kick out every transnational elite for whom national borders are seen as merely obstacles to the flow of cheap goods and labor.

People have fought wars for less than you can achieve with your vote.

People have crossed oceans for less than you can achieve with your vote.

And let me be clear about something else. This election is not about partisan politics—it's not a race about the differences between Republican or Democratic policies.

This is an election about entirely different philosophies.

On the one side, you have Ryan's philosophy, which governs only to the benefit of a small few: the corporate executives whom he meets in banquet rooms, the lobbyists at the Chamber of Commerce, his donors in Silicon Valley with whom he shares a good chuckle at your expense.

And on the other side, you have our philosophy, which believes in governing for the benefit of all the people—a philosophy that believes in representing every working mom, dad, student, grandparent, and every single person who calls themselves an American.

A vote for this philosophy is a vote on behalf of every person who will never sit in a boardroom with Goldman Sachs executives. It's a vote for every person who will never go out for steak dinners at four-star restaurants with Chamber of Commerce lobbyists. It's a vote for every person who will never visit Denmark or Brussels with foreign bureaucrats and plot and plan how to rule.

To the Wisconsin voter who asks for nothing more than a secure job, a safe community, and a representative who will fight for them—I ask for your vote, because that is what I can deliver and that is what I promise. My one and only loyalty is to you and no one else.

Can you name one time when Paul Ryan fought as hard for you and your family as he's fought for corporate America?

I'd like to read you something from a man named Dan Golvach.

Dan's twenty-five-year-old son, Spencer, was murdered by an illegal immigrant. Spencer was stopped at a red light when his killer decided to use Spencer's head as target practice. Dan reminds us that "this wasn't Syria or Iraq. It was the neighborhood I grew up in."

On Father's Day, Dan asked Paul Ryan to accompany him to the place where Dan will spend every Father's Day for the rest of his life—his son's grave. Dan wrote, "This way Speaker Ryan can see firsthand what pandering to the cheap illegal labor lobby means to Americans who can't afford to put a security fence up around their house."

But Paul Ryan ignored Dan's plea.

Last summer, Kate Steinle's father came to Washington. He told Congress how "help me, Dad" were the last words he'd ever hear from his daughter, as she lay dying in his arms. And he begged Congress to take action.

Five months after her death, Paul Ryan voted to reward sanctuary cities with federal grants.

Today, I'm calling on Paul Ryan to release the names of the corporate lobbyists he's working with on immigration—the lobbyists who mean more to Ryan than the American fathers and mothers, who have buried their American children as a result of our nation's open borders.

Today, I am calling on Paul Ryan to live under the same conditions which he's imposed upon our American communities . . .

Paul Ryan, if you will not build a border wall for America, then I am asking you to tear down your wall. If you will not build a wall to honor the mothers and fathers of the dead, if you will not build a wall to protect our children, then, sir, you should tear down your wall and show everyone that you will live under the same conditions as they do.

People like Paul Ryan and Mark Zuckerberg love open borders so long as they stop at the property lines to their mansions. They ensconce their families with walls and fences, but then lecture us about how we have to be more charitable. And lecture us about how America "is more than our borders."

Don't let one more American child die because Paul Ryan won't secure the border. Your vote on August 9 can save a life.

APPENDIX 2

THE LITTLE GIRL SPEECH

Somewhere out there in America tonight, it may be in a place like Kenosha or Janesville, or a faraway community—it could be a big city or a small town, a mother will be putting her little girl to bed. And that little girl will dream about all the things she'll do when she grows up.

Maybe the little girl is Latino; maybe she's African-American; maybe she is white; maybe she is Asian—it doesn't matter. What matters is that she's an American girl, and she

THE LITTLE GIRL SPEECH

can do anything she wants.

Maybe she'll be a doctor, or a lawyer, or an accountant, or a police officer.

Maybe she'll dream of having children of her own one day.

But that little girl won't get to live those dreams because our politicians—led by House Speaker Paul Ryan—have failed in their most fundamental and sacred obligation: to provide safety for us by securing our border and enforcing our immigration laws.

And so, that child will be the next victim, of the thousands of victims, of our open borders. Maybe she'll be killed by an illegal immigrant in a car crash, or a home invasion, or a vicious violent assault—the kind that happens to men and women all across this country each year.

As this mother puts her child to sleep, she has no idea that her daughter will be the next Kate Steinle or Sarah Root.

Out there tonight, all across this country, is the next Jamiel Shaw Jr., the next Brandon Mendoza, the next Spencer Golvach Jr.— the next American child who won't get to live out their American dream because Paul Ryan believes that his family deserves a border wall, but you don't.

This is not hyperbole. This is not exaggeration. This is reality.

I have been honored and privileged and humbled to spend time with the mothers who have lost their beautiful American children to illegal immigrant violence enabled by sanctuary cities, which Paul Ryan has funded, and allowed in by open borders that Paul Ryan has left open—children killed by open borders, that have boosted profits for Paul Ryan's donors and makes all of us less safe—a cause to which Paul Ryan has devoted his entire professional life.

Ryan smirks and looks down at us from his high station and has the audacity to complain that the mothers of children killed by illegals have dared to ask him for an audience.

He has gone to the media and his payroll pundits and has condemned the mothers for doing so.

Has he thought for one moment about their loss or considered their suffering?

Aren't they entitled to a meeting with him even though they don't have billions of dollars or an army of lobbyists or well-known names?

Every day, all across this country, there is some American that wakes up believing that anything is possible for them in this great country of ours, only to have those dreams brought to a brutal and violent end because our politicians don't have the decency, or courage, or desire to protect the lives of innocent Americans.

So understand this: With your one vote, you can save the life of the next Kate Steinle.

With your one vote, you can save the life of an American child from becoming the next statistic. You can save the next forgotten name, the next forgotten victim.

With your one vote, you can save that next American parent from having to live out the rest of their life in sorrow and grief. You can save the next person from becoming the next obituary—the next mother from having to demand that her politicians secure the border so the next American child doesn't have to die too.

How many thousands of Americans have to lose their lives to fund the career of Paul Ryan?

Ask yourself this question—think hard and be honest: Has

Paul Ryan ever cared as much about the lives of these Americans as he's cared about furthering his political career?

Has he ever fought as hard for these Americans as he's fought for his budget-busting omnibus, or as he's fought for his disastrous trade deal, or corporate handouts?

Paul Ryan would rather cut benefits for U.S. veterans than cut benefits for illegal immigrants.

He doesn't represent the people of Wisconsin; he represents Wall Street donors.

He is not merely a symptom of the corrupt and broken system; he is the corrupt and broken system.

And his appeal to you now in the name of loyalty or unity or togetherness comes from a man who has shown no loyalty to the American people; a man who has displayed no unity with our fallen brothers and sisters; a man who has demonstrated no desire to bring us together in shared prosperity.

Rarely before in history have a people been given such an opportunity to affect such profound change as Wisconsin voters have in this open primary.

All we have to do is cast one ballot on August 9.

With your one vote you can stop amnesty for good.

With your one vote you can stop TPP.

With your one vote you can end rule by corporations.

You can end the corruption, the corporatism, the kickbacks.

You can end the serfdom to special interests and become free and safe and secure.

You have the chance to prove to the special-interest globalists, the pundits, and the professional politicians that they don't control your life, that they don't control your vote, and that you're not going to fall for their glossy lies and slick ads, but instead vote the truth and vote your conscience.

With your one vote you can give hope to those who will never have enough money to attend one of Ryan's wealthy donor dinners, but who are Americans and are entailed to equal representation and protection under the law.

One vote to save the lives of innocent Americans.

One vote to save Wisconsin.

One vote to save America.

Next Tuesday, declare your independence.

Let August 9 be Wisconsin's Independence Day.

Thank you so much for joining me today.

CONCESSION SPEECH AS A CALL TO ACTION

Thank you. Thank you all so much.

I'm so glad to see you all, and I'm especially glad to see all of the reporters here tonight because I have a profoundly important message for our district and for our nation that I need to share with you.

But before that, I just have a few very brief comments.

First, tonight we defied everyone's expectations for this campaign.

Just the fact that you are all here tonight demonstrates that our message played across our district and the country, despite the desires of our opponents, and despite their corporate buddies' efforts to silence us.

Our success is a testament to each and every one of you.

I believe, a little perspective is in order here.

We took on the leader of the world's globalist movement.

When you take on Paul Ryan, you are not just taking on Paul Ryan.

You are taking on the Chamber of Commerce, you are taking on the Koch brothers, you are taking on Wall Street, and you are taking on all of the transnational elites who will do anything to keep their Speaker in Congress.

Let us consider how others have fared before us.

Since his reelection bid in 2000, Paul Ryan has never faced a real primary challenge. He has essentially run unopposed for nearly twenty years.

Historically, U.S. representatives from Wisconsin are rarely ever challenged. One report observed that, "from 1950 through 2014, less than one in five Wisconsin U.S. representatives faced a primary challenger."[1]

Since 1950, only one Wisconsin U.S. representative has ever lost his primary. We were up against a 99.7 percent success rate, but we took on the challenge.

We took on the challenge because we knew that, despite the odds, we could not continue to be quiet, and sit down, and watch as we were led by a man who does not only look down upon our desires, but actively fights against them at every turn.

We know how the people of our district and our state feel. We've seen the polls.

We know that seven out of ten Republican Wisconsinites favor a pause in Muslim migration.

We know a majority of Wisconsin Republican voters reject Ryan's trade agenda.

We know that nine in ten Republican voters oppose Ryan's plan to increase immigration.

We cannot be led by a leader who stands against us and against our interests.

We can't be led by a leader who busts the budget at every available opportunity.

A leader who tried to ram through the job-destroying Trans-Pacific Partnership agreement, which will dissolve U.S. sovereignty.

A leader who— on the single issue of greatest importance to our base, immigration—is on the side of Luis Gutiérrez.

A leader who promises his wealthy donors at exclusive retreats that he will "repudiate" the views of his conservative base.

If Nancy Pelosi stood opposed to over 90 percent of her electorate on an issue of great importance to them, she would not be a leader in her party.

We cannot be led by someone who does not represent our values and our principles.

Paul Ryan is able to buy his elections and gets political cover from corporate media.

Corporate media wants Ryan in power because they know that he will do their bidding.

Isn't it interesting that the national media, which attacks Ryan mercilessly in the general election for wanting to cut Medicare and social security, is suddenly his greatest friend in the primary?

Why might that be?

Because Paul Ryan is the Republican they need to accomplish their agenda.

They need Paul Ryan to keep borders open. They need Paul Ryan to pass multinational trade deals. They need Paul Ryan to be a useful foil, the corporate crony that they can use to caricature all Republicans and win elections in the end. They get all the benefits that come from their policies of soulless globalism, and Republicans—as a result of Paul Ryan—get all of the blame for human suffering and misery that accompanies it.

How many times has Paul Ryan met with the Chamber of Commerce? How many times has he met with the executives of Facebook, Microsoft, and Google? How many times has he met with a lobbyist for a global outsourcing firm, or large international corporation?

Now consider—how many times with the victims of illegal immigrant violence? Or the border agents? Or ICE officers? Or the workers forced to train their foreign replacements brought in on guest worker visas?

Ask yourself this question—when Disney workers were laid off, and were forced to be silent as they had to train their foreign replacements, did Paul Ryan race to the House floor to condemn Disney's action?

Did he bring forth legislation to fix it?

Did he command the news cycle every day until we got justice for our American workers?

Or did he continue his sleep doll routine of being the Republican caricature that the Left so badly wants—saying the same old things you've heard a million times before about Medicare and social security reform and tax reform, while real flesh-and-blood human beings watch their dreams die and disappear not merely in spite of their American citizenship, but because of their American citizenship? A direct discrimination against American citizens.

How has it reached this point that we've let Americans be killed by open borders; that we have let factories be shipped wholesale overseas because we've refused to enforce the most basic terms of our trade agreements, or have refused to protect ourselves against illicit trading practices, which are an act of economic warfare against us?

And our leaders—led by Ryan himself—just don't do nothing, but they aid and abet our economic destruction.

How many arms has Ryan twisted behind the scenes to push his donor's agenda?

Ryan twisted every last arm to pass his omnibus bill to bring in more foreign workers to slave as groundkeepers and hotel maids to bring down the price of labor just a little bit for his corporate friends.

He poured his sweat into passing that bill just to make labor just a little bit less expensive for corporations.

And yet he couldn't lift a finger to save one American job.

He couldn't put the same energy or passion into demanding the construction of a border wall, or protections for American labor, or demanding new rules to ensure that foreign workers can't be exploited, or to protect American standards of living for the American people.

No. We are all helpless in Paul Ryan's race to the bottom so he can crown a new glorious achievement for his donors.

Ask yourself: are you not entitled to a leader that represents your views?

You want less immigration—are you not entitled to leaders who want the same?

You want a security wall across the border—are you not entitled to leaders who want the same?

You want people who overstay visas to be deported—are you not entitled to leaders who want the same?

You want wages protected for American workers—are you not entitled to leaders who want the same?

You want trade deals that create jobs and manufacturing here at home—are you not entitled to leaders who want the same?

Why should you be resigned to this permanent servitude to Ryan's special-interest desires? Why should you have to beg and plead—like a child to a parent—for your congressman and Speaker to help you, when he should instead be lifting his voice to the heaven every day on your behalf?

That is what you deserve as your sacred birthright as an American.

You deserve a leader who is as loyal to you as you are to your children, your country, and your God in heaven.

Now, look—what we have accomplished here tonight is historic beyond words and measure, because we have lit the spark of a raging fire of righteous populism that will lift up the spirit of the nation. A movement that will put the hopes and fears and aspirations of American citizens first before any consideration.

As a result of our campaign, people know where Ryan stands. The mask has been pulled off, the charade is over, sentiment behind the smirk has been revealed, and the con is up.

They know who he cares about.

They know who he fights for.

And it has never, and it will never be, all of you.

We all know what Ryan's agenda means.

It means that our border will never be secured.

It means that immigration will never be reduced.

It means the rights of American citizens will never be protected.

Ryan has not merely allowed the immigration crisis to take place; he has not simply socialized at lavish diners in your time of need; he has not simply hid behind his personal border wall while denying you yours.

He has created the crisis. He has spurned your need and your want. And he's done everything in his power to deny you the security that is your absolute right.

Twenty years ago, Ryan began his campaign against the American worker. Twenty years ago, he fought to keep our border open and he has done so every day since then.

Any time there was a fork in the road where Ryan could choose between security or amnesty, prosperity or poverty, country or corporations—he has chosen the latter every single time.

Mark it down and remember it now: as long as Ryan is House Speaker, immigration will never be cut, dangerous migration from the Islamic world will never be reduced, trade deals will never be fixed, and the onslaught of globalism will never, ever stop until it has wiped out every last shred of independence in this land. . . .

Until we are nothing more than just another location in the global marketplace, in which your culture, values, heritage and your brotherhood and sisterhood means nothing.

In which black Americans, white Americans, Latino and

Asian Americans are all second-class Americans because they are not corporations and because they're not a foreign worker and because they are not a lobbyist or a politician.

I will continue fighting until every American—whether they be black or white or Latino, what have you—can be first-class citizens in their country again.

In my closing speech to the voters of Wisconsin ahead of the election, I talked about a girl—a daughter just like one of the millions of daughters to parents all across this America—the millions of daughters in this country who are entitled to grow up in safety and peace, just like every son and child in this country.

We have to keep that American girl from becoming the next Kate Steinle and that American son from becoming the next Joshua Wilkerson, the next innocent life lost because politicians like Paul Ryan will not fight with every breath to keep that child safe from the ravages of open borders and criminal cartels that don't belong in our cities, in our district, or in our country.

We will save that life—not as many as we'd like, and not as many as we could have saved if we had won this race, but we will save thousands of lives and restore millions of dreams. And that is because we will ultimately succeed.

And we will succeed because we know that the truth is the one thing in this world that can never be destroyed.

There is no amount of money in Paul Ryan's bank that can cause a lie to kill a truth, a falsehood to kill a fact, a smear to kill honest statement of principle.

The truth, once set free as it has been in this campaign, only grows each day like a righteous avalanche as it becomes faster and stronger and ultimately unstoppable. Until the people of this country have been liberated from leadership that is unworthy of the name. And new leadership emerges composed exclusively of the people and working exclusively for the people.

And it begins, my friends, with the people in this room tonight.

So I ask you this question. Are you prepared to carry on with me tomorrow, and next week and two years from now to liberate this district from Paul Ryan? And to free this country from its failed leaders? And to replace this soulless globalism with a new Americanism? A new Americanism that respects the inherent worth and dignity of each and every person in this land? I am with you. I will be with you if you will join me every step of the way.

Thank you for your friendship. Thank you for your devotion. And thank you for joining me in this great American journey. God bless you, and good night.

NOTES

CHAPTER 1: THE WAR ROOM

1. John Q. Public, "The Ryan Budget Epitomizes How Washington Views Veterans," *JQP* (the John Q. Public blog), December 22, 2013, https://www.jqpublicblog.com/the-right-thing/.

2. AC/DC, "Moneytalks," by Angus Young and Malcolm Young, in *The Razor's Edge*, Atco Records and Albert/EMI, 1990.

3. Matthew Boyle, "Ryan-Murray Budget Deal in Shambles," Breitbart, February 11, 2014, http://www.breitbart.com/big-government/2014/02/11/ryan-budget-deal-in-shambles/.

CHAPTER 3: BORDER WARS

1. Joe Caponi, "Rudy Giuliani Addresses VARBusiness 500 Crowd," CRN, June 15, 2005, http://www.crn.com/news/channel-programs/164303446/rudy-giuliani-addresses-varbusiness-500-crowd.htm,

2. John Adams, "Novanglus Essays No. 7," https://en.wikisource.org/wiki/Novanglus_Essays/No._7.

3. Gerald Ford, "Quotations; The Words of Gerald Ford," New York Times, December 27, 2006, http://www.nytimes.com/2006/12/27/washington/28fordquotescnd.html

4. Daniel Harper, "Obama Admits: 'I Just Took an Action to Change the Law,' Weekly Standard, November 25, 2014 http://www.weeklystandard.com/obama-admits-i-just-took-an-action-to-change-the-law/article/820167

5. Jacob Bojesson, "Is Trump Wrong about a Border Wall? One Stunning Chart Has the Answer," *Daily Caller*, March 26, 2016, http://dailycaller.com/2016/03/26/is-trump-wrong-about-a-border-wall-one-stunning-chart-has-the-answer/.

6. Jason Beaubien, "Drug Cartels Prey on Migrants Crossing Mexico," NPR, July 7, 2011, http://www.npr.org/2011/07/07/137626383/drug-cartels-prey-on-migrants-crossing-mexico.

7. Kelly Riddell. "Sheriffs Warn of Violence from Mexican Cartels Deep into Interior of U.S." *Washington Times*, April 9, 2014. http://www.washingtontimes.com/news/2014/apr/9/sheriffs-warn-of-violence-from-mexican-cartels-dee/.

8. Veronique de Rugy, "The Biggest Beneficiaries of the Ex-Im Bank," Mercatus Center at George Mason University, April 29, 2014, https://www.mercatus.org/publication/biggest-beneficiaries-ex-im-bank.

9. Ibid.

10. Mike Flynn. "Export-Import Bank Rescued by Speaker Paul Ryan's Highway Bill," Breitbart, November 5, 2015, http://www.breitbart.com/big-government/2015/11/05/export-import-bank-rescued-speaker-paul-ryans-highway-bill/.

11. "Final Vote Results for Roll Call 576: H R 597," House.gov, October 27, 2015, http://clerk.house.gov/evs/2015/roll576.xml

12. Logan Beirne, "Don't Buy the Denials, Puerto Rico Is Being Bailed Out," RealClearMarkets, May 31, 2016, http://www.realclearmarkets.com/articles/2016/05/31/puerto_rico_is_a_bailout_by_any_other_name_102192.html.

13. See Martin Guzman, "Wall Street's Worst Vulture Hedge Funds Are Making a Killing by Undermining the Global Economy," Quartz, June 17, 2016, https://qz.com/707165/wall-streets-vulture-hedge-funds-are-making-a-killing-by-undermining-the-global-economy/.

14. Rep. Paul Ryan, "Top 20 Industries Contributing to Campaign Cmte," OpenSecrets.org, accessed April 10, 2017, https://www.opensecrets.org/politicians/industries.php?cycle=2016&cid=N00004357&type=I&newmem=N.

15. Julia Hahn, "PBS Documentary: House Freedom Caucus Founder Was Key to Paul Ryan, Luis Gutierrez Open Borders Effort," Breitbart, October 26, 2015, http://www.breitbart.com/big-government/2015/10/26/pbs-documentary-house-freedom-caucus-founder-key-paul-ryan-luis-gutierrez-open-borders-effort/.

16. Jim Hoft, "Paul Ryan to Hispanic Audience: House Will Vote on Citizenship in October," *Gateway Pundit*, July 26, 2013, http://www.thegatewaypundit.com/2013/07/paul-ryan-tells-hispanic-audience-house-will-vote-on-citizenship-in-october/.

17. "UN Working with Islamist Group to Resettle over 15,000 Syrian Refugees in America," *Investor's Business Daily*, November 17, 2015, http://www.investors.com/politics/editorials/why-is-un-using-islamist-group-to-resettle-syrian-refugees-in-the-us/.

18. Leo Hohmann. "FBI: No Way to Screen 'Refugees' Coming to U.S., WND, October 22, 2015, http://www.wnd.com/2015/10/fbi-no-way-to-screen-refugees-coming-to-u-s/.

19. Ann Corcoran. "What Does the Refugee Resettlement Program Cost US Taxpayers?" Refugee Resettlement Watch, October 29, 2014, https://refugeeresettlementwatch.wordpress.com/2014/10/29/what-does-the-refugee-resettlement-program-cost-us-taxpayers/.

20. Michael Patrick Leahy, "Unholy Alliance: Christian Charities Profit $1 Billion Fed Program to Resettle Refugees, 40 Percent Muslim," Breitbart, November 29, 2015, http://www.breitbart.com/big-government/2015/11/29/unholy-alliance-christian-charities-profit-1-billion-fed-program-resettle-refugees-40-percent-muslim/.

21. "LYING MEDIA: Front Page @CNN Article by @KFile LIES BY OMISSION about Islam to Imply Steve Bannon Is a Bigot," GotNews, January 31, 2017, http://gotnews.com/lying-media-front-page-cnn-article-kfile-lies-omission-islam-imply-steve-bannon-bigot/.

22. Bob Unhuh, "FBI expert: Quran is 'revealed word of God'," June 4, 2013, WND, http://www.wnd.com/2013/06/fbi-expert-quran-is-revealed-word-of-god/.

23. "DHS Agent: West Blind to 'Jihad through Immigration,'" WND, June 7, 2017, http://www.wnd.com/2016/06/dhs-agent-west-blind-to-jihad-through-immigration/.

24. Hadith 1:35, http://www.sacred-texts.com/isl/bukhari/bh1/bh1_34.htm.

25. Tiffany Gabbay, "Morsi's Anti-Semitic 'Apes and Pigs' Comment Wasn't Take out of Context, It Was Taken out of the Quran," TheBlaze, January 24, 2013, http://www.theblaze.com/contributions/morsis-anti-semitic-apes-and-pigs-comment-wasnt-taken-out-of-context-it-was-taken-out-of-the-quran/.

26. Sahih Muslim, Book on Government, chapter 47, https://sunnah.com/muslim/33/226.

27. Russell Berman. "Paul Ryan (Again) Rejects Trump's Muslim Ban," *Atlantic*, June 14, 2016, https://www.theatlantic.com/politics/archive/2016/06/paul-ryan-again-rejects-trumps-muslim-ban/486992/.

28. Abby Hamblin, "Read George W. Bush's Speech to Muslims after 9/11," *San Diego Union-Tribune*, January 31, 2017, http://www.sandiegouniontribune.com/opinion/the-conversation/sd-george-w-bush-on-islam-20170131-htmlstory.html.

29. Bob Unruh, "Pope: 'Authentic Islam Opposes Violence," WND, November 26, 2013, http://www.wnd.com/2013/11/pope-authentic-islam-opposes-violence/.

30. Matt O'Brien, "Government Insider: 'Immigration Vetting System Badly Broken,'" ImmigrationReform.com, October 7, 2016, http://immigrationreform.com/2016/10/07/government-insider-immigration-vetting-system-badly-broken/.

31. John Hayward. "Seven Inconvenient Facts about Trump's Refugee Actions," Breitbart, January 29, 2017, http://www.breitbart.com/big-government/2017/01/29/trumps-immigration-pause-sober-defenses-vs-hysterical-criticism/.

32. Allan Smith, "Paul Ryan Says He Might Sue Donald Trump If He Tried to Enact the Muslim Ban," *Business Insider*, June 17, 2016, http://www.businessinsider.com/paul-ryan-donald-trump-sue-muslim-ban-2016-6.

33. Julia Hahn, "Flashback: Paul Ryan Fully Funds Obama's Visas for 300,000 Muslim Migrants in Single Year," Breitbart, June 17, 2016. http://www.breitbart.com/2016-presidential-race/2016/06/17/flashback-paul-ryan-fully-funds-obamas-visas-300000-muslim-migrants/.

CHAPTER 4: TRADE WARS

1. As quoted in the University of Michigan's *University Chronicle*, March 27, 1869, books.google.de.

2. "China Average Yearly Wages 1952-2017," Trending Economics, http://www.tradingeconomics.com/china/wages.

3. Kevin Kearns, "Full TPP Text Reveals a Very Bad Deal for America," Breitbart, November 5, 2015, http://www.breitbart.com/big-government/2015/11/05/full-tpp-text-reveals-a-very-bad-deal-for-america/.

4. Ian Kullgren, "Yes, Clinton Did Call TPP the 'Gold Standard,'" *The Politico Wrongometer* (blog), October 9, 2016, http://www.politico.com/blogs/2016-presidential-debate-fact-check/2016/10/yes-clinton-did-call-tpp-the-gold-standard-229501.

5. Robert E. Scott, "U.S.-Korea trade deal Resulted in Growing Trade Deficits and More Than 95,000 Lost U.S. Jobs," *Working Economics Blog*, May 5, 2016, http://www.epi.org/blog/u-s-korea-trade-deal-resulted-in-growing-trade-deficits-and-more-than-95000-lost-u-s-jobs/.

6. Julie Pace and Steve Peoples, "Trump Names Lawyer Lighthizer as Top Trade Rep," AP, January 3, 2017, http://bigstory.ap.org/article/ed546adec4d248eaadc66271e25e7912.

7. Sundance, "It's Officially Official – Donald Trump Wins Electoral College Vote…," Conservative Treehouse, December 19, 2016, https://theconservativetreehouse.com/2016/12/19/its-officially-official-donald-trump-wins-electoral-college-vote/.

8. Trevor Timm. "The TTIP and TPP Trade Deals: Enough of the Secrecy," *Guardian*, May 4, 2016, https://www.theguardian.com/commentisfree/2016/may/04/ttip-tpp-trade-deals-secrecy-greenpeace-leak.

9. Alex Swoyer, "Ryan's 'Misperceptions' on Trade Deal Unveiled, Reports Suggest," Beitbart, June 17, 2015, http://www.breitbart.com/big-government/2015/06/17/ryans-misperceptions-on-trade-deal-unveiled-reports-suggest/.

10. Adam Behsdui, "Obama Puts Congress on Notice: TPP Is Coming," Politico, August 12, 2016, http://www.politico.com/story/2016/08/obama-congress-trade-warning-226952.

11. Lydia DePillis, "Everything You Need to Know about the Trans-Pacific Partnership," *Washington Post*, December 11, 2013, https://www.washingtonpost.com/news/wonk/wp/2013/12/11/everything-you-need-to-know-about-the-trans-pacific-partnership/?utm_term=.19926057459b.

12. The Trans-Pacific Partnership Agreement Implementation Act (draft), https://ustr.gov/sites/default/files/DRAFT-Statement-of-Administrative-Action.pdf.

13. Eric Schneiderman, "Don't Let TPP Gut State Laws," *Politico* magazine, April 19, 2015, http://www.politico.com/magazine/story/2015/04/trans-pacific-partnership-state-laws-117127.

CHAPTER 5: AMERICA'S TRADITION OF ECONOMIC NATIONALISM

1. Ben Shapiro, "Trump's Anti-'Globalism' Is Anti–Free Trade," *National Review*, June 29, 2016, http://www.nationalreview.com/article/437277/donald-trump-free-trade-isnt-globalism.

2. Alexander Hamilton, Report on Manufactures, December 5, 1791, http://www.constitution.org/ah/rpt_manufactures.pdf.

3. Thomas J. DiLorenzo, "Lincoln's Tariff War," Mises Institute, May 6, 2002, https://mises.org/library/lincolns-tariff-war.

4. Robert Lighthizer, "Lighthizer: Donald Trump Is No Liberal on Trade," *Washington Times*, May 9, 2011, http://www.washingtontimes.com/news/2011/may/9/donald-trump-is-no-liberal-on-trade/.

5. Clyde Farnsworth, "U.S. Raises Tariff for Motorcycles," *New York Times*, April 2, 1983, http://www.nytimes.com/1983/04/02/business/us-raises-tariff-for-motorcycles.html.

6. "New Deal Trade Policy: The Export-Import Bank & the Reciprocal Trade Agreements Act, 1934," State Department Office of the Historian: Milestones 1921–1936, accessed March 10, 2017, https://history.state.gov/milestones/1921-1936/export-import-bank.

7. From the Historical Statistics of the United States Series 1790–1945 and the White House Historical Tables 1940–2016.

8. "United States-Canada Automotive Products Agreement," Hearings Before the Committee on Ways and Means, House of Representatives, Eighty-Ninth Congress, April 27, 28, and 29, 1965, http://www.stewartlaw.com/Content/Documents/HR%20-%20United%20States-Canada%20Automotive%20Products%20Agreement.pdf.

9. Jack Hervey, "Canadian–U.S. Auto Pact—13 Years After," Federal Reserve Bank of Chicago, accessed March 10, 2017, https://www.chicagofed.org/~/media/publications/economic-perspectives/1978/ep-jul-aug1978-part4-hervey-pdf.pdf.

10. *The Canada–U.S. Free Trade Agreement*, Government of Canada, accessed March 10, 2017, http://www.international.gc.ca/trade-agreements-accords-commerciaux/assets/pdfs/cusfta-e.pdf.

11. "Israel Free Trade Agreement," Office of the United States Trade Representative, accessed March 19, 2017, https://ustr.gov/trade-agreements/free-trade-agreements/israel-fta.

12. "U.S.- Israel Free Trade Area Agreement," Trade Agreement Compliance program, accessed March 19, 2017, http://tcc.export.gov/trade_agreements/exporters_guides/list_all_guides/exp_005529.asp.

13. Joe Ogrinc, "The NAFTA Analysis: Not Free Trade," FEE: Foundation for Economic Education, May 1, 1993, https://fee.org/articles/the-nafta-analysis-not-free-trade/.

14. Sunny Freeman, "NAFTA's Chapter 11 Makes Canada Most-Sued Country Under Free Trade Tribunals," *Huffington Post*, January 14, 2015, http://www.huffingtonpost.ca/2015/01/14/canada-sued-investor-state-dispute-ccpa_n_6471460.html.

CHAPTER 6: THE WAR ON SOVEREIGNTY

1. See TPP Final Table of Contents, https://ustr.gov/trade-agreements/free-trade-agreements/trans-pacific-partnership/tpp-full-text.

2. Preamble, accessed April 11, 2017, https://ustr.gov/sites/default/files/TPP-Final-Text-Preamble.pdf.

3. TPP, chapter 27, "Administrative and Institutional Provisions," https://ustr.gov/sites/default/files/TPP-Final-Text-Administration-and-Institutional-Provisions.pdf.

4. TPP, chapter 28, "Dispute Settlement," p. 28-2, https://ustr.gov/sites/default/files/TPP-Final-Text-Dispute-Settlement.pdf.
5. Alan Farnham, "Seafood from Asia Raised on Pig Waste, Says News Report," ABC News, October 17, 2012, http://abcnews.go.com/Business/consumers-eating-feces-tainted-shrimp-fish-seafood-asia/story?id=17491264.
6. TPP, chapter 28, "Dispute Settlement," p. 28-13.
7. TPP, chapter 20, "Environment," p. 20-4, https://ustr.gov/sites/default/files/TPP-Final-Text-Environment.pdf.
8. Henry Lamb. "UN's Agenda 21 Is in Your Community," WND, April 23, 2011, http://www.wnd.com/2011/04/290225/.
9. "An RNC Resolution to Commend the Nation of Israel for Its Relations with the United States of America," GOP.com, January 13, 2012, https://cdn.gop.com/docs/2012_wintermeeting_resolutions.pdf.
10. Andrew Follett, "Obama Administration Ramps Up Legal Fight Against Fracking," Daily Caller, March 23, 2016, http://dailycaller.com/2016/03/23/obama-adminstration-ramps-up-legal-fight-against-fracking/.
11. Colin Chilcoat, "After Years of Fracking, What Do We Know?" OilPrice.com, March 18, 2016, http://oilprice.com/Energy/Crude-Oil/After-Years-of-Fracking-What-do-We-Know.html.
12. "TPP: Made in America—Environment," Office of the United States Trade Representative, accessed March 10, 2017, https://ustr.gov/sites/default/files/TPP-Chapter-Summary-Environment.pdf.

CHAPTER 7: THE WAR ON AMERICAN WORKERS

1. Seung Min Kim, "Trade Pact Foes: Deal Could Cause Flood of Immigrants," Politico, May 5, 2015, http://www.politico.com/story/2015/05/conservatives-trade-pact-could-cause-flood-of-immigrants-117620.
2. TPP, chapter 10, "Cross-Border Trade in Services," art. 10.5.a.iv, https://ustr.gov/sites/default/files/TPP-Final-Text-Cross-Border-Trade-in-Services.pdf, p. 10-5.
3. Alex Swoyer, "TPP Trade Deal Hits U.S. Immigration in 'a Massive Way,'" Breitbart, November 6, 2015, http://www.breitbart.com/big-government/2015/11/06/tpp-trade-deal-hits-u-s-immigration-law-massive-way/.
4. John Miano, "Former Abbott Labs Workers Meet in Chicago," Center for Immigration Studies, April 26, 2016, http://cis.org/miano/former-abbott-labs-workers-meet-chicago.
5. TPP, chapter 12, "Temporary Entry for Business Persons," p. 12-2, https://ustr.gov/sites/default/files/TPP-Final-Text-Temporary-Entry-for-Business-Persons.pdf,

CHAPTER 8: THE WAR ON INTELLECTUAL PROPERTY

1. TPP, chap. 18, "Intellectual Property," sec. A, art. 18.2, https://ustr.gov/sites/default/files/TPP-Final-Text-Intellectual-Property.pdf; emphasis added.

2. http://portal.uspto.gov/pair/PublicPair.

3. "Advancing U.S. Economic Interests in Asia: Hearing Before the Committee on Foreign Affairs, House of Representatives," May 14, 2015, https://www.gpo.gov/fdsys/pkg/CHRG-114hhrg94606/pdf/CHRG-114hhrg94606.pdf, 27.

4. Ibid.

5. Ibid., 27–28.

6. Ibid, 33–34.

7. Ibid, 34–35.

CHAPTER 9 : OBAMACARE, RYANCARE, AND WHAT THE GOP SHOULD DO ON HEALTH CARE

1. George Rasley, "Puerto Rico Bailout Shows Corruption of Paul Ryan and Establishment GOP Leadership," Conservative HQ, April 14, 2016, http://www.conservativehq.com/article/22873-puerto-rico-bailout-shows-corruption-paul-ryan-and-establishment-gop-leadership.

2. Sean Moran, "Biggest Insurance Company in Obamacare Exchanges Rallies Behind Ryan's Obamacare 2.0," Breitbart, March 10, 2017, http://www.breitbart.com/big-government/2017/03/10/biggest-insurance-company-obamacare-exchanges-rallies-behind-ryans-obamacare-2-0/.

3. Philip Bump, "President Trump's Health-Care Plan Probably Would Make Health Care Pricier for Core Trump Voters," *Washington Post*, March 8, 2017, https://www.washingtonpost.com/news/politics/wp/2017/03/08/president-trumps-health-care-plan-would-likely-make-health-care-pricier-for-core-trump-voters/?utm_term=.911a078cb95e.

4. Katie McHugh, "7 Reasons Why Obamacare 2.0 Is All but Guaranteed to Impose Crushing Costs on Voters, Hurt Trump's Base and Hand Power Back to the Democrats," Breitbart, March 10, 2017, http://www.breitbart.com/big-government/2017/03/10/7-reasons-why-obamacare-2-0-is-all-but-guaranteed-to-impose-crushing-costs-on-voters-hurt-trumps-base-and-hand-power-back-to-the-democrats/.

5. Max Greenwood, "Trump: ObamaCare Replacement Will Get 'Rid of State Lines' for Insurance," *The Hill*, March 7, 2017, http://thehill.com/policy/healthcare/322669-trump-obamacare-replacement-will-get-rid-of-state-lines-for-insurance.

6. Sean Moran, "CBO: Full Repeal of Obamacare Insures More Americans Than Ryan's Obamacare-Lite Plan," Breitbart, March 14, 2017, http://www.breitbart.com/big-government/2017/03/14/cbo-full-repeal-of-obamacare-insures-more-americans-than-ryans-obamacare-lite-plan/.

7. John Walsh, "What Will Happen to Health Insurance in 2017? Doctors Say Repeal Obamacare, but Don't Replace It," *International Business Times*, January 13, 2017, http://www.ibtimes.com/what-will-happen-health-insurance-2017-doctors-say-repeal-obamacare-dont-replace-it-2473295.

8. Philip Klein, "CBO Score Makes the Case for Full Repeal and Free Market Replacement," *Washington Examiner*, March 14, 2017, http://www.washingtonexaminer.com/cbo-score-makes-the-case-for-full-repeal-and-free-market-replacement/article/2617290.

9. Matthew Boyle, "Honeymoon Over: Speaker Paul Ryan Targets His Own Republicans, Not Democrats, with Ads on Health Care," Breitbart, March 9, 2017, http://www.breitbart.com/big-government/2017/03/09/honeymoon-speaker-paul-ryan-targets-republicans-not-democrats-ads-healthcare/.

10. "The Fiscal Burden of Illegal Immigration on United States taxpayers (2013)," Federation for American Immigration Reform, http://www.fairus.org/publications/the-fiscal-burden-of-illegal-immigration-on-united-states-taxpayers.

11. Stephen Dinan, "Nearly 20 Million Illegal Immigrants in U.S., Former Border Patrol Agents Say," *Washington Times*, September 9, 2013, http://www.washingtontimes.com/news/2013/sep/9/nearly-20m-illegal-immigrants-us-ex-border-patrol/.

12. David North, "How Employers Cheat America's Aging by Hiring Foreign Workers," Center for Immigration Studies, June 2012, http://cis.org/Employers-Cheat-Aging-By-Hiring-Foreign-Workers-Spanish.

13. Ibid.

14. Katie McHugh, "Obamacare 2.0 Guts Enforcement, Gives Illegal Aliens Health Care Through Identity Fraud," Breitbart, March 7, 2017, http://www.breitbart.com/big-government/2017/03/07/obamacare-2-0-guts-enforcement-gives-illegal-aliens-healthcare-through-identity-fraud/.

15. Ann Coulter, "A Health Care Plan So Simple, Even a Republican Can Understand!" *Ann Coulter* blog, March 29, 2017, http://www.anncoulter.com/columns/2017-03-29.html#read_more.

CHAPTER 10: AN AMERICAN FIRST FOREIGN POLICY

1. Lucas Tomlinson, "3 US Soldiers Shot in Afghanistan 'Insider Attack,' Fox News, March 19, 2017, http://www.foxnews.com/world/2017/03/19/3-us-soldiers-shot-in-afghanistan-insider-attack.html

2. John Quincy Adams, quoted in "She Goes Not Abroad in Search of Monsters to Destroy," *American Conservative*, July 4, 2013, http://www.theamericanconservative.com/repository/she-goes-not-abroad-in-search-of-monsters-to-destroy/.

3. Rowan Scarborough, "Saudi Government Funded Extremism in U.S. Mosques and Charities: Report," *Washington Times*, July 19, 2016, http://www.washingtontimes.com/news/2016/jul/19/911-report-details-saudi-arabia-funding-of-muslim-/.

4. Russell Goldman, "'You Are the Future of Europe,' Erdogan Tells Turks," *New York Times*, March 17, 2017, https://www.nytimes.com/2017/03/17/world/europe/erdogan-turkey-future-of-europe.html?_r=0.

5. Aaron Klein, "Turkey 'Providing Direct Support' to ISIS," WND, October 9, 2014, http://www.wnd.com/2014/10/turkey-providing-direct-support-to-isis/.

6. Glenn Greenwald, "Key Democratic Officials Now Warning Base Not to Expect Evidence of Trump/Russia Collusion," *Intercept*, March 16, 2017, https://theintercept.com/2017/03/16/key-democratic-officials-now-warning-base-not-to-expect-evidence-of-trumprussia-collusion/.

7. Art Moore, "Yes, There *Are* 'No-Go' Zones in Europe," WND, January 20, 2015, http://www.wnd.com/2015/01/yes-there-are-no-go-zones-in-europe/.

8. Michael Patrick Leahy, "Six Diseases Return to US as Migration Advocates Celebrate 'World Refugee Day,'" Breitbart, June 19, 2016, http://www.breitbart.com/big-government/2016/06/19/diseases-thought-eradicated-world-refugee-day/.

9. "American Courts Creating 'Affirmative Right to Immigrate,'" WND, March 16, 2017, http://www.wnd.com/2017/03/american-courts-creating-affirmative-right-to-immigrate/.

10. Paul Bedard, "Report: 72 Convicted of Terrorism from 'Trump 7' Mostly Muslim countries, *Washington Examiner*, February 11, 2017, http://www.washingtonexaminer.com/report-72-terrorists-came-from-7-muslim-countries-trump-targeted/article/2614582#.WKAkWjMX4CQ.twitter.

11. "Can Your U.S. citizenship Be Revoked?," FindLaw, accessed March 20, 2017, http://immigration.findlaw.com/citizenship/can-your-u-s-citizenship-be-revoked-.html.

12. "An Explanatory Memorandum on the General Strategic Goal for the Group in North America," hosted by the Center for Security Policy, accessed March 20, 2017, https://www.centerforsecuritypolicy.org/wp-content/uploads/2014/05/Explanatory_Memoradum.pdf.

13. Leo Hohmann, "Plaintiff Behind Trump Travel Ban Runs Muslim Brotherhood," WND, March 16, 2017, http://www.wnd.com/2017/03/plaintiff-behind-trump-exec-order-ban-runs-muslim-brotherhood-mosque/.

14. Rahul Sastry and Bennett Siegel, "The French Connection: Comparing French and American Civilian Nuclear Energy Programs," *Stanford Journal of International Relations* 11, no. 2 (Spring 2010), https://web.stanford.edu/group/sjir/pdf/Nuclear_11.2.pdf.

CHAPTER 11: THE NEW RIGHT, THE NEW MEDIA, AND A TRUMP GOP

1. Matthew Boyle, "Panic Mode: Khizr Khan Deletes Law Firm Website That Specialized in Muslim Immigration," Breitbart, August 2, 2016, http://www.breitbart.com/2016-presidential-race/2016/08/02/khizr-khan-deletes-law-firm-website-proving-financially-benefits-pay-play-muslim-migration/.

2. Seung Min Kim, "McConnell, Ryan Defend Khans amid Trump Remarks," Politico, July 31, 2016, http://www.politico.com/story/2016/07/khan-mconnell-trump-226485.

3. Reposted in Julia Hahn, "Donald Trump Thanks Paul Nehlen for Support After Ryan Sides with Hillary Clinton," Breitbart, August 1, 2016, http://www.breitbart.com/2016-presidential-race/2016/08/01/donald-trump-thanks-paul-nehlen-support-ryan-sides-hillary-clinton/.

4. Sam Levine and Daniel Marans, "Donald Trump Goes After Grieving Mother Of Killed American Soldier," July 30, 2016, http://www.huffingtonpost.com/entry/donald-trump-ghazala-khan_us_579d0bb5e4b08a8e8b5e57d1.

5. Clare Foran, "The Curious Case of Khizr Khan's 'Travel Privileges,' *Atlantic*, March 7, 2017, https://www.theatlantic.com/politics/archive/2017/03/khizr-khan-travel-canada-trump/518862/.

6. Letter reprinted by Breitbart and reposted in "Ryan's Security Force Refuses to Deliver Ryan Letters from Victims of Open Borders," TeaParty.org, July 25, 2016, https://www.teaparty.org/ryans-security-force-refuses-deliver-ryan-letter-victims-open-borders-178238/.

7. Julia Hahn, "ICE Union Head Savages House Speaker Paul Ryan on Out of Control Illegal Immigration," Breitbart, August 5, 2016, http://www.breitbart.com/big-government/2016/08/05/ice-union-head-savages-house-speaker-paul-ryan-on-out-of-control-illegal-immigration/.

8. Nick Gass, "Trump: GOP Will Become 'Worker's Party,' under Me, Politico, May 26, 2016, http://www.politico.com/story/2016/05/trump-gop-workers-party-223598.

9. Matthew Conlen, "The Last 10 Weeks of 2016 Campaign Stops in One Handy Gif," FiveThirtyEight, December 16, 2016, https://fivethirtyeight.com/features/the-last-10-weeks-of-2016-campaign-stops-in-one-handy-gif/.

CONCESSION SPEECH AS A CALL TO ACTION

1. Eric Ostermeier, "Why a 2016 Tea Party Primary Challenge Against Paul Ryan Will Fail," Smart Politics, January 7, 2016, http://editions.lib.umn.edu/smartpolitics/2016/01/07/why-a-2016-tea-party-challenge-against-paul-ryan-will-fail/.

INDEX